Uncommon Valour

Uncommon Valour

1916 & the Battle for the South Dublin Union

PAUL O'BRIEN

MERCIER PRESS
IRISH PUBLISHER – IRISH STORY

MERCIER PRESS

Cork

www.mercierpress.ie

Trade enquiries to CMD BookSource,
55a Spruce Avenue, Stillorgan Industrial Park,
Blackrock, County Dublin

ISBN: 978 1 85635 654 1

10 9 8 7 6 5 4 3 2 1

A CIP record for this title is available from the British Library

Printed and bound in the EU.

Contents

DEDICATED TO
DR LIAM DISKIN, MD
1944–2005

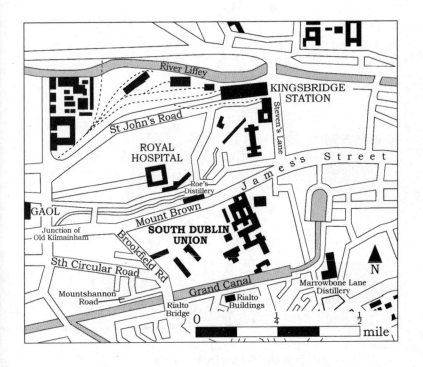

River Liffey

KINGSBRIDGE
STATION

St John's Road

Steven's Lane

ROYAL
HOSPITAL

James's Street

Roe's
Distillery

GAOL

Mount Brown

SOUTH DUBLIN
UNION

Junction of
Old Kilmainham

Brookfield Rd

Sth Circular Road

Grand Canal

Marrowbone Lane
Distillery

N

Mountshannon
Road

Rialto
Bridge

Rialto
Buildings

0   ¼   ½

mile

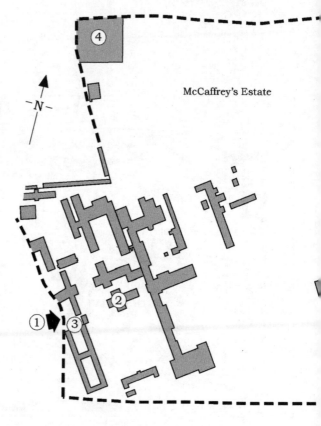

Map of the South Dublin Union

(1) Rialto entrance

(2) R.C. Church

(3) Auxiliary Workhouse

(4) Ceannt's forward position

(5) Infirmary where Nurse Keogh was shot and where the Volunteers were chased from ward to ward

(6) Matron's House

(7) Canal entrance

(8) Convent

(9) Wards through which British soldiers travelled

(10) Nurses' Home and Headquarters of the 4th Battalion

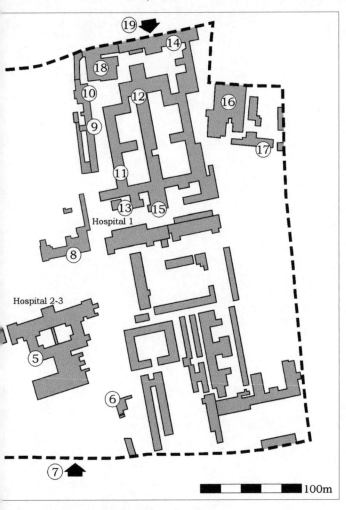

100m

(11) Wards occupied by British soldiers during frontal assault on the Nurse's Home

(12) Dining Hall. Ground floor occupied by British soldiers during the conflict

(13) Cul-de-sac

(14) Front of South Dublin Union. Boardroom with administrative offices on first floor. Occupied by volunteers 1916

(15) R.C. Church

(16) Laundry

(17) Mortuary

(18) Bakehouse

(19) Main Gate

Acknowledgements

This book would not have been possible without the help of Professor Davis Coakley of St James's Hospital, Dublin, who was so generous with his time. By walking the grounds of the hospital, Professor Coakley brought the battlefield to life, an action I hope to recreate within these pages.

Grateful thanks are once again due to the staff of the National Library, Dublin, National Archives, Military Archives at Cathal Brugha Barracks, Dublin, University College Dublin Archives, Kilmainham Gaol Archives, the Library of the Office of Public Works, The Allen Library, Carlow County Library, Guinness Ireland Archives and the staff of the Sherwood Forester Museum.

I am indebted to Elizabeth Gillis for research on the Irish Volunteers, to Sue Sutton and Roger E. Nixon for their research in the British Military Archives at Kew in London, Michael Ó Doiblín for photography, Gerry Woods for cartography and to Andrew D. Hesketh and Dr Mike Briggs for material on the Sherwood Foresters.

For supporting the idea and reading the initial drafts, a special word of thanks to Dr Mary Montaut.

I would like to thank the following for their insight, support and encouragement: Cyril Wall, Henry Fairbrother, Ray Bateson, John McGuiggan, James W. Taylor, Eoin Purcell, John Morton, Martin Lyons, Tony Checkley, William Henry, Maureen Burke, Dr Barbara Smyth, Loretto Diskin and Phil Fitzpatrick.

I would like to thank and all at Mercier Press in particular Wendy Logue, whose perceptive editing has made such a difference.

Finally I would like to thank my fiancée Marian and my parents who have had to grow used to countless recitations of military facts and figures that may have seemed boring to them but were all-important to me. They have at all times given me sound advice and encouragement when it was needed.

This book has been written using available historical records both in Ireland and in England.

There are many people who helped with this book and in naming some of them I can only apologise to those who I fear I may have indirectly forgotten and I would like to invite them to make me aware of any omissions or relevant information that may be included in any future updated edition.

My thanks are due to all those who provided help and information in the course of writing this book.

Foreword

I, like many people, have found myself a patient in St James's Hospital, Dublin. Travelling through the maze of buildings and corridors one cannot help but notice the change in architectural features as modern hospital architecture becomes intertwined with pre-twentieth-century stone buildings. I was curious to find out about the history of these older buildings and in the course of my investigation discovered that one of the few urban battlefields that still exists intact may be found in the grounds of St James's.

St James's Hospital started life as a poorhouse constructed in 1667, becoming a foundling hospital in 1727. In the early nineteenth century the hospital was closed and the structure then became a workhouse called the South Dublin Union, a place for Dublin's destitute, infirm and the insane. The complex was spread over fifty acres and consisted of an array of buildings that in April 1916 housed 3,282 people, including patients, doctors, nurses and ancillary staff. The area, enclosed within a high stone wall, consisted of living quarters, churches, an infirmary, a bakery, a morgue, acres of green space and many stone hospital buildings connected by a labyrinth of streets, alleyways and courtyards.

After the Irish Civil War in 1923, the complex continued to develop as a municipal hospital and the name was changed to St Kevin's Hospital. In the late 1960s plans were made to amalgamate many of the voluntary infirmaries in Dublin and St Kevin's became known as St James's Hospital in 1971.[1]

It was during the 1916 Easter Rising that this compound was to become one of the landmarks of the fight for Irish independence. After the implementation of the Act of Union in 1801, which abolished the Irish Parliament, Ireland was directly ruled from Westminster. In the years that followed, Home Rule became the main objective of Irish nationalists, but it wasn't until a century later, in 1914, after decades of violence and political agitation, that the third Home Rule Bill was finally enacted for all but the north-east of the country. However, the bill's implementation was postponed by the outbreak of the First World War. For many Irish nationalists this delay was unacceptable and their aim soon became full independence from Britain.[2]

On Easter Monday 1916, the everyday existence of the South Dublin Union was shattered. Members of the

Irish Volunteers and the Irish Citizen Army, consisting of 1,500 men, women and teenage boys and girls, mobilised to declare an Irish republic independent from the British Empire. At this time the British Empire was the largest in the world, comprising a quarter of the world's land surface as well as a quarter of its population, making it a massive opponent for the small band of Irish Volunteers. However, the majority of the Empire's military might was focused on the First World War, thus providing the Irish insurgents with their best chance of success.

On Easter Monday, 24 April 1916, members of the 4th Battalion of the Irish Volunteers under the command of Commandant Éamonn Ceannt occupied the site of the South Dublin Union. During the week that followed, Dublin, like Stalingrad, Berlin and more recently Sarajevo, became an urban battlefield. The South Dublin Union was one of the main focal points of the fighting in the city, until its forces finally surrendered on Patrick Pearse's orders on Sunday 30 April.

The battle for the South Dublin Union was complicated and poses a number of questions to the student of military history. Questions arise in relation to the military strategy and tactics deployed by the British army, and whether the South Dublin Union could have been overrun and taken by the British at the beginning of the week. The failure to consolidate early gains meant that later in the week traumatised and inexperienced troops of the Nottingham and Derbyshire regiments, having suffered heavy casualties at the hands of the Irish Volunteers during the battle for Mount Street Bridge, found themselves once again in action against a determined foe, resulting in further casualties on both sides.

With regard to the Irish side, questions arise in relation to Eoin MacNeill's countermanding order, an action that left the ranks of the Volunteers seriously under strength, as well as why a controversial order was issued that resulted in the evacuation of their headquarters during Thursday's battle, leaving one man to single-handedly repulse a British attack and save the day. By examining the problems experienced by both the defenders and the attackers, it becomes clear that both sides faced significant obstacles which are as relevant in modern warfare as they were in 1916. The method of urban warfare that was employed during the battle of the South Dublin Union is instructive to modern armies and is often adapted in twenty-first-century conflicts such as Afghanistan and Iraq.

In recent years the regeneration of Dublin city has eroded many of the remnants of Easter 1916. There have been attempts by various organisations to try to conserve those buildings linked with the conflict because they represent a wealth of the nation's history. The architectural heritage within St James's Hospital is an irreplaceable expression of the sacrifice and diversity of our past. Personal histories and events of that week have left their mark on these places and they should be preserved for posterity.

A full and detailed account of the defence and the attack on the South Dublin Union has never been penned and it is in memory of the men on both sides who fought, lived and died in Dublin city during Easter week 1916 that this book has been written.

Chapter 1

Easter Monday, 24 April 1916
Morning

On the morning of Easter Monday, 24 April 1916, at 11 a.m., members of the 4th Battalion of the Irish Volunteers mobilised at Emerald Square, Dolphin's Barn, in Dublin city. A number of Volunteers who had assembled at Larkfield in Kimmage earlier that morning, marched to the square, arriving at 11 a.m., but even so the battalion was seriously under strength. This was due to an order issued by Eoin MacNeill and published on Sunday 23 April countermanding a previous order for all Volunteer groups to assemble that day. MacNeill's order read:

Owing to the critical position, all orders given to the Irish Volunteers for tomorrow, Easter Sunday, are

hereby rescinded and no parades, marches or other
movements of the Irish Volunteers will take place.
Each individual Volunteer will obey this order strictly
in every particular.[3]

MacNeill, Chief-of-Staff of the Irish Volunteer Force,
withdrew his support for the Rising having heard that
Roger Casement had been arrested and that the *Aud*, a
German ship laden with arms and ammunition for the
Volunteers, had been intercepted by the Royal Navy.
The Rising originally planned for Easter Sunday now
looked to be in jeopardy, hence MacNeill's actions, but
the military council of the IRB decided to go ahead
on Easter Monday instead. As a result of MacNeill's
countermanding order, the number of Volunteers who
eventually did mobilise around the country was much
smaller than if it had taken place as planned on Easter
Sunday. Only 120 Volunteers mobilised out of the 4th
Battalion's full strength of 700.

Éamonn Ceannt, the officer in command of the
4th Battalion, was thirty-five years old. A member of
the Provisional Government and a signatory of the
Proclamation, he was employed by Dublin Corporation
and married with a young son. A fluent Irish speaker
and an accomplished uilleann piper, he held the rank
of commandant in the Irish Volunteers. Ceannt was a

thoroughly efficient officer, respected by his men for his leadership and military expertise.

At 11.35 a.m. the battalion moved out in two parties. The plan was to occupy the South Dublin Union workhouse as battalion headquarters, along with three strategically located outposts: Roe's Distillery in Mount Brown, Watkins' Brewery at Ardee Street and Jameson's Distillery at Marrowbone Lane. Ceannt led the first group, which consisted of a dozen cyclists and a few Volunteers on foot, along the banks of the Grand Canal towards the Rialto entrance at the rear of the South Dublin Union. The Volunteers, many of them in uniform, were armed with a variety of weapons including Mauser rifles from the Howth landing, British-issue short magazine Lee-Enfield rifles, shotguns, revolvers and automatic pistols.

Lieutenant William Thomas Cosgrave led the second group. In order to avoid detection by the authorities, this main group of Volunteers was led through a warren of side streets until they reached the front gates of the South Dublin Union. Lieutenant Cosgrave was thirty-six years old, a Dublin city councillor and a local man. Accompanying him was forty-two-year-old Vice-Commandment Cathal Brugha. Born Charles Burgess at Richmond Avenue, Dublin, on 18 July 1874, Brugha was educated at the Colmcille Schools in Dublin and later Belvedere College. Invigorated by the Gaelic renaissance of the early twentieth century, Brugha began to look at the nation's heroic past. Immersing himself in Irish culture, he became a fluent Gaelic speaker. A man of great vigour he was driven by a relentless determination and his position as vice-commandant of the 4th Battalion would be crucial in the coming days. He was known as a patriot and soldier dedicated to the cause of Irish independence.

As this second group marched to its destination, small parties detached from the main column and took up their posts along the route. Each outpost consisted of an officer and about twenty Volunteers: Captain Con Colbert was detailed to Watkins' Brewery in Ardee Street, Captain Seamus Murphy took up position at Jameson's Distillery in Marrowbone Lane and Captain Thomas McCarthy occupied Roe's Distillery in Mount Brown. These positions were chosen with the aim of preventing British troops from entering the city from the south-west. It was planned that military movements could be checked and halted along the quays of the River Liffey, at Kingsbridge Railway Station (now Heuston Station), and at the headquarters of the British commander-in-chief in Ireland, the Royal Hospital, Kilmainham. Ceannt knew that British reinforcements would be dispatched from Richmond barracks, Islandbridge barracks and the Royal barracks. Others would come from Britain's largest camp, the Curragh, via train from County Kildare. The South

Dublin Union and its outposts were a major defensive position in the south-west of the city.

Ceannt entered the Union through a small door at Brookfield Road, Rialto. The only resistance he met was that of the gatekeeper who was pushed aside and relieved of his keys. The phone lines were cut and nine Volunteers under the command of Captain George Irvine were deployed to secure the Rialto entrance. These Volunteers occupied a corrugated iron structure (Auxiliary Workhouse) that faced the large gate (3). This building was used to house the male mental patients of the Union. It was 300 feet long, twenty-six feet wide and divided into six dormitories by wooden partitions that were connected by narrow corridors. The Volunteers entered the structure through the porch entrance facing the Catholic church. The ward-master and patients were directed to a place of safety at the rear of the sixth dormitory. Permission was granted to staff who wanted to leave the area. Captain Irvine instructed his men to fortify their position, which they proceeded to do, using mattresses, chairs, tables and bed ends to reinforce the walls of the corrugated building. One Volunteer proceeded to dig a slit trench in front of the gate.

Arriving late, Volunteer James Burke and brothers James and Paddy Morrissey found the Rialto gate already barricaded, so they scrambled over the wall and reported to Captain Irvine. They assisted in barricading the windows that faced the wall over which they had climbed. Having prepared their position they took up their posts facing Mountshannon Road, vigilant and ready for the impending attack.

After leaving Captain Irvine, Ceannt proceeded half a mile through the grounds to the front gate of the Union. Here he joined with the main force led by Cathal Brugha that had entered through the main gate at James's Street.

The Volunteers quickly occupied the offices above the arched gateway that fronted onto James's Street (14). Within this block of buildings was the South Dublin Rural District Council office with the boardroom above. The building also contained administration offices and wards. At the end of this block was the paint shop and adjacent to this was the Nurses' Home (10). Volunteers, including James Foran, began barricading the windows with leather-bound ledgers. In order to allow them to traverse the building without leaving cover, they began tunnelling through the adjoining internal walls that were eighteen inches thick. Each building was to become an impregnable fortress.

Shortly afterwards the main gate was opened to allow a horse and cart to enter. Having spoken with Ceannt, the driver removed the horse's harness and departed. The gate was then locked and barricaded. The dray was laden with homemade hand grenades, supplies of barbed wire, shovels, picks and other equipment, and was quickly unloaded. It was then overturned and used as a barricade in front of the church that was opposite the main gate. Boxes and bags were filled with clay from the garden borders to make improvised sandbag defences that reinforced the position.

Dr McNamara, the resident medical practitioner, approached the Volunteers to protest about their actions. Having received no satisfaction from them, he then entered an office building and picked up the telephone receiver in order to alert the authorities to their actions. Volunteer James Coughlan confronted the doctor and ordered him to put down the telephone. He refused and Coughlan then prodded him with the bayonet on his rifle. McNamara turned to Coughlan and threatened: 'I'll get your name and give it to the ...' He left the sentence unfinished as other Volunteers arrived in the office and began to dismantle the phone while Coughlan kept him under guard.[4]

A series of garden huts located within the compound near the main gate had been earmarked to be Ceannt's command post. However, it soon became evident that the small force of Volunteers available would be unable to defend the entire entrance area from this position. Lieutenant Cosgrave noted that the Nurses' Home (10) would be a suitable alternative defensive position. Situated at a right angle to James's Street, this granite, three-storey structure had a dominating view of James's Street and the Union's entrance courtyard. From the rear of the building one could look out across the entire Union complex. The officers decided that this position would make a better battalion headquarters and it was soon occupied – windows were smashed and barricades were erected. Brugha detailed a number of men to take up positions at the windows that looked out across McCaffrey's Estate at the rear and beyond to the Rialto gate. At the front of the building other Volunteers looked out onto the main entrance courtyard and stood ready.[5]

Within the Union, officials and hospital staff remained at their posts and nurses removed the patients to safer quarters. Red Cross flags were draped from the windows of the buildings that still held staff and patients. Throughout the week the work of the institution continued, despite the chaos.

In order to prevent his position within the South Dublin Union from being outflanked, Ceannt ordered two parties of Volunteers to occupy sections of McCaffrey's Estate, a large green area of eight to ten acres within the Union grounds. Lieutenant William O'Brien, Section Commander John Joyce and three other Volunteers took up an advance position at the junction of Mount Brown and Brookfield Road (4). McCaffrey's Estate was a series of irregular elevations that tapered steeply down to Mount Brown. The Volunteers' post dominated the road leading from Old Kilmainham to James's Street and they concealed themselves behind a low wall. Another officer and eight Volunteers took up position behind a hedgerow at the upper end of the field, nearer the rear wall of the Nurses' Home.

Ceannt also sent one officer and five men to defend the canal wall at the rear of the Union. High walls made the east, or city side, of the Union immune to attack, and because of this Ceannt decided not to post Volunteers on this side of the complex.

About 250 yards from the Rialto entrance was Hospital 2–3 (5), a building that was occupied by eight Volunteers, two on the ground floor and six on the upper floor. Volunteers Dan McCarthy and Jim Kenny took up positions on the ground floor at the front. They had been told not to worry about the rear of the building, as the Volunteers in the Marrowbone Lane Distillery would have this covered. Captain Douglas fFrench Mullen began organising the rest of the group on the second floor. McCarthy later recalled an amusing incident in which Captain fFrench Mullen asked, 'Where are the trenching tools?' A little shovel was produced. When fFrench Mullen saw it he said, 'It doesn't matter.' He knew they would not be able to break through the eighteen-inch thick walls with such an implement.[6]

When Volunteer Peadar Doyle entered the convent building (8), a surprised nun enquired if he had come to read the gas meters. He politely replied, 'No, sister, but we are in a hurry.'[7]

As Ceannt organised his defences he could hear the sound of military music reverberating through the air from Richmond barracks in Inchicore. 'They don't know yet,' remarked Ceannt. Suddenly the music stopped, as the barracks was notified of the Rising. The men in the South Dublin Union braced themselves for an imminent attack.

Chapter 2

Easter Monday, 24 April 1916
Noon

At noon on Easter Monday, 24 April 1916, the British detachment at Richmond barracks in Inchicore received an urgent communiqué from garrison headquarters at Dublin Castle. It ordered all troops in barracks to proceed to the Castle fully armed. The 3rd Battalion of the Royal Irish Regiment was stationed at Richmond barracks under the command of Lieutenant Colonel R.L. Owens. At this time the regiment consisted of eighteen officers and 385 other ranks. This reserve battalion was used to supply reinforcements to the battalions on active service and consisted of men drawn from newly trained recruits, as well as officers and men returning from sick leave. As the regiment was being mustered, a picket of 100 men who were kept in constant readiness, prepared to leave the barracks. Troops made ready and were issued with a supply of ammunition. A telephone message was received informing the regiment that 'Sinn Féiners' had occupied the General Post Office in Sackville Street. Major Holmes, the officer in command of the picket, was ordered to proceed towards the Castle with caution.[8]

At approximately 12.40 a.m., Major Holmes halted his column at the Kilmainham crossroads. In the distance he could clearly see a group of Irish Volunteers leaning over the wall of McCaffrey's Estate at the junction of Mount Brown and Brookfield Road (4). His advance guard, consisting of one sergeant and five soldiers who were 150 yards ahead of the column, was allowed to pass the Volunteer's position unchallenged and continue onwards to the city.

Major Holmes then ordered Lieutenant George Malone with a company of twenty men to follow the route of the advance guard and proceed towards Dublin Castle. Their rifles were unloaded as this was the proper procedure when operating in the city. They marched off in columns of four down the middle of the road. Some of the soldiers were recent recruits from County Tipperary, while others were veterans, having already seen action on the Western Front. Lieutenant Malone ordered his men to load their weapons. Clips were inserted into their rifles and slapped in tight with the palms of their hands. They then pulled back the bolt to slide a round into the chamber and checked the safety catch. When they were within five yards of the junction, a volley of shots rang out from the Volunteers' position. Three of Lieutenant Malone's men collapsed as they were hit. Some of the soldiers stood their ground and attempted to return fire, while others made for cover.

From his position behind the wall in McCaffrey's Estate (4), Volunteer Section Commander John Joyce took aim and squeezed the trigger of his rifle. His target was the figure of a sergeant who was directing his men to cover. He fired and missed. The sergeant stood his ground. Joyce reloaded and fired again, but the bullet struck a brick wall above the sergeant's head. The sergeant used the butt of his rifle to break open a door into a tan-yard and the men fell through the entrance into relative safety. As Lieutenant Malone rushed towards the open door, the soldier in front of him was hit and fell to the ground. Malone grabbed at the man's collar and attempted to pull him through the doorway, but while doing so he was himself hit. Malone staggered through the doorway and into the yard. He shouted orders to his men while reloading his revolver. He heard a voice stating, 'the officer is hit', before he collapsed.[9] When he regained consciousness, two women were bandaging his wound. Lieutenant Malone surveyed the yard and saw Private Moulton with his jaw shattered. His men looked shaken, but had taken up positions at the windows and door, and were returning a steady rate of fire.

In the return of fire by the British, Volunteer John Owens was mortally wounded. He came from the Coombe area of Dublin city. He worked as an artificial limb maker and was twenty-four years old. Two other Volunteers were also wounded in this exchange of fire.

As suddenly as the skirmish began it came to a stop. There was an uneasy lull in the fighting for almost fifteen minutes as British troops manoeuvred into position in preparation for an attack.

At the junction of Old Kilmainham and O'Connell Road, Lieutenant Colonel R.L. Owens witnessed the assault on his men. He immediately called up the remainder of the battalion from Richmond barracks, planning to attack the South Dublin Union in force. Assisted by his adjutant, Captain Roche Kelly, Lieutenant Colonel Owens sent a company to the Royal Hospital in Kilmainham, the residence of the commander-in-chief of the British armed forces in Ireland. The south range of this three-storey building dominated the grounds of the South Dublin Union. His men ran up the oak staircases and took up firing positions in the many dormer windows that overlooked McCaffrey's Estate. A Lewis machine-gun was deployed on the roof in order to lay down covering fire in the forthcoming attack. The automatic machine-gun was fed from a drum magazine that held forty-seven rounds. Operated by a two-man team, the cyclic rate of fire could be 550 rounds per minute. Using this weapon the British army had evolved a 'rushing tactic' – covered by the Lewis gun – a section or platoon could move forward a short distance and then provide covering fire for the original unit. This tactic was continuously used during the battle for the South Dublin Union.

Lieutenant Colonel Owens directed Major E.F. Milner to take two companies and make a flank attack by way of the Rialto entrance (1) and the Grand Canal. Two experienced officers, Captain Alfred Ernest Warmington and Lieutenant Alan Livingston Ramsay, both of the Royal Irish Rifles, assisted him. Captain Warmington was the son of Alfred Warmington, the manager of the Munster and Leinster Bank in Naas, County Kildare. A veteran of the Boer War in South Africa, he had also served in France during the early months of the Great War. Lieutenant Ramsay was commissioned as a lieutenant in the Royal Irish Rifles on 15 August 1914. His family conducted a successful nursery business from their home in Ballsbridge supplying plants and flowers throughout the city. At twenty-six years of age, Ramsay was a veteran of the Western Front and had been wounded in action there.

Their detachment proceeded down O'Connell Road and onto the South Circular Road. The Volunteers' position at the Rialto gate of the Union could be seen ahead. In order to cover the attack, Major Milner deployed a number of men into positions on the upper floors of the houses that stood opposite the Rialto gate (1). He also directed fifteen men to take up firing positions at the windows in the Rialto buildings on the other side of the canal as these structures overlooked the southern area of the Union. The remainder of his men took up positions on the road opposite the Rialto gate and prepared for the order to storm the Union. Word went down the line and the men moved rapidly into their firing positions without making any noise.

At 12.55 p.m. the assault began. The uneasy silence was shattered as British troops opened fire. The Lewis machine-gun located in the Royal Hospital enfiladed the Volunteers located in McCaffrey's Estate. The crash of rifle fire and the staccato rattle of the machine-gun warned Volunteer Lieutenant William O'Brien of how vulnerable his position in McCaffrey's Estate was. Realising the danger, O'Brien ordered his men to retreat. He shouted 'spread out, spread out' as they ran back towards the hospital buildings across the open field, devoid of any cover. The only way to return to the command area or the nearest auxiliary hospital building, the Catholic Women's

Hospital (11) was to move rapidly and try to use the dips and slight ridges in the field as cover. As the Volunteers withdrew from their position, John Joyce could hear men cry out as they were hit. Richard O'Reilly was shot and killed as he crossed the field. Each Volunteer ran in short rushes from one point to another, hoping the bullets would miss. Occasionally they turned and fired wildly at an unseen enemy. As Joyce crawled forward looking for cover, the dirt ahead of him jumped, spat and then exploded in geysers of earth as bullets kicked up the soil. After almost an hour and a half of crawling through the field, Joyce and the surviving Volunteers reached the relative safety of the Women's Hospital. They were also near the convent that lay just fifty yards from Hospital 2–3 (5).

The Volunteers at the Rialto gate (1) heard the noise of rapid gunfire in the distance. Suddenly a barrage of covering fire was laid down on their corrugated hut. Within seconds the hut resembled a sieve, as the bullets entered and ricocheted around the inside of the building. The patients in dormitory 6 cowered on the ground as the bullets ripped through the structure. The ward-master's coat was pierced as he tried to protect the patients. Volunteer John Traynor was mortally wounded and fell to the floor. Traynor had been employed as a messenger boy in the nearby Guinness Brewery and, at seventeen years of age, he was the crack shot of the company. The others moved to his side and for a brief moment, prayed for the repose of his soul.

Captain Irvine sent a messenger to Ceannt at headquarters requesting further orders. The messenger returned to Irvine with a written dispatch that stated he should retire his force further into the Union grounds. This order was impractical as the British assault was growing more intense and Irvine sent the Volunteer messenger back to Ceannt to relay this message to him. The messenger succeeded in reaching Ceannt, but as the fighting then intensified he was unable to return to Irvine. The unit at Rialto was now cut off from the central command in the Union.

In the meantime, Captain Warmington ordered fifty men to use the wall of the Union as cover and move towards the rear of the site, along the route of the Royal Canal, and attempt to gain entry to the grounds via the rear entrance (7). They moved across the road on the double and set off.

The covering rifle fire enabled Lieutenant Ramsay to lead the first assault on the Rialto gate. The gate was heavily barricaded and locked. Ramsay abandoned the idea of forcing open the main gate and his unit moved under the wall of the Union for cover. Here they located a small wooden door that they quickly broke down. As Lieutenant Ramsay charged through the doorway a volley of shots from the Volunteers met him. Ramsay was shot through the head and fell on the roadway near the chapel (2). His men withdrew back out through the gate onto the street. A brief truce followed and the Volunteers permitted a stretcher party to collect the body of the fallen officer.

On receiving the news about the young lieutenant's death, Captain Warmington was consumed with rage. He ordered his men to line up and he himself led another charge through the narrow entrance. He was shot dead as he entered the doorway and under intense fire his men broke off their attack and retreated. A second ceasefire was called and another stretcher party collected Warmington's corpse. His body was laid on the pavement beside that of Lieutenant Ramsay. The fight then continued.

In the corrugated hut at the Rialto gate the situation was becoming desperate. The British covering fire from the Rialto buildings and the houses opposite the gate was intense and the din was ear-shattering and unnerving. Captain Irvine realised his section was isolated and the position untenable, and in a last desperate attempt to get orders, he decided to send Paddy Morrissey to Volunteer headquarters at the Nurses' Home. As Morrissey left the hut, their post came under heavy fire. Within minutes he crawled back through the door, blood pouring from a wound in his leg. The Volunteers attempted to return fire, but were under attack from all sides. The superior firepower of the British army had enabled them to move closer. The metal corrugated hut became a hothouse of explosions, smoke, vibrations and the bitter smell of burning gunpowder. The Volunteers now realised they were surrounded. James Burke and Willie Corrigan fired desperately as the khaki-clad enemy moved into range. Corrigan received a wound to the eye as bullets shattered the glass windows of the hut. Both men were covered in blood, but continued to fight on furiously. Soon, with their weapons overheating, the Volunteers had to take turns stopping fire to allow their rifles to cool.[10]

The door of the hut was well barricaded. Members of the Royal Irish Regiment prepared to make an assault on the door using a large, iron lawnmower as a makeshift battering ram. Three British soldiers charged the door with the makeshift device and as it crashed open, soldiers poured in through the breach shouting: 'Put up your hands and surrender.' Hopelessly outnumbered and outgunned, the Volunteers reluctantly surrendered and were led out of the Union at gunpoint. Captain George Irvine, Jimmy Morrissey, Willie Corrigan, Seán Dowling and James Burke were taken to Kilmainham police station. Paddy Morrissey, whose leg had been shattered, was escorted to hospital.

With the fall of the Rialto gate, the British crown forces had secured an access point into the Union grounds.

However, they still had to cross open terrain in order to attack Ceannt's other positions within the complex. Commandant Ceannt and his men would ensure that every inch of the South Dublin Union would be contested, a tactic that resulted in no quarter being given by either side.

Chapter 3

Easter Monday, 24 April 1916
Afternoon

A squad of British troops was moving up along the southern wall of the Union, parallel to the canal. They planned to gain access to the Union grounds via the rear entrance (7) and sweep northwards towards the front entrance, clearing buildings of insurgents as they advanced. However, as they attempted to force open the southern gate, they came under a barrage of fire from the Volunteers in the Marrowbone Lane Distillery.

From his position on the top floor of the distillery, Volunteer Robert Holland was able to dominate the surrounding area for miles. He fired rapidly into the ranks of the soldiers who had taken up position at the Union's southern gate. The large number of soldiers had made an easy target for Holland. Armed with a Howth Mauser rifle and a Lee Enfield rifle, he fired continuously into the ranks of the British soldiers. Josie O'Keeffe, a member of Cumann na mBan, the women's organisation which worked closely with the Irish Volunteers, loaded the weapons and handed them to Holland, who used them with deadly accuracy.[11]

Caught in the open, the troops took cover along the bank of the canal and returned fire. Heavy casualties were inflicted on the attacking force and their dead and wounded littered the canal bank. A number of soldiers, pinned down by the accurate fire, attempted to scale the nine-foot wall that surrounded the Union. One soldier who managed to climb the wall, took up position behind a telegraph pole. As he raised his rifle to fire he was hit. His body fell from the wall and bounced off the canal bank before splashing into the water. An officer sitting on the wall, revolver in hand, was shot through the head and died instantly.

Within the grounds of the Union, the six Volunteers positioned within the inner wall at the canal entrance (7) found themselves under intense fire from the British troops positioned in the upper rooms of the Rialto buildings.

After several attempts, and despite their losses, the British troops forced open the back gate and entered the Union grounds. At 2.30 p.m. approximately fifty British troops fanned out and moved towards the main gate to where Ceannt had established his headquarters. The advancing troops were joined by those who had stormed the Rialto entrance. However, Hospital 2–3 stood in their way (5).

The Volunteers who held the southern wall were in danger of being outflanked. Unable to hold their position, they retreated towards Hospital 2–3. In their desperate attempt to withdraw, eighteen-year-old Brendan Donelan was hit and mortally wounded. A native of Loughrea he had been employed in the drapery trade. He lay in the open, bleeding to death. Volunteer James Quinn was also shot and killed, leaving a wife and young family. A painter by trade, he was a member of the Colmcille Hurling Club and was often heard to say that he would exchange his camán for nothing but a rifle.

The advancing British soldiers quickly lost their way among the labyrinth of buildings and were delayed by the confusing intersecting alleyways and avenues. Passing beneath the occupied windows, the unsuspecting soldiers were fired upon by the Volunteers, who then quickly withdrew and reformed in another area to repeat this type of attack.

From the second floor of Hospital 2–3 (5), bursts of rapid rifle fire erupted, catching the advancing British troops in open ground. The British soldiers took cover and returned fire, aiming at the puffs of black smoke emitting from the windows. Running in short rushes, some soldiers succeeded in reaching the wall of the building. Using a pass key they gained entrance to the hospital's inner courtyard.

On the ground floor of Hospital 2–3, Volunteers Dan McCarthy and Jim Kenny found themselves confronted by a large force of British soldiers. They opened fire and then ran, locking a door between themselves and their pursuers. The British troops returned fire, then smashed open the door and gave chase to their attackers. McCarthy and Kenny ran through dormitories and down narrow corridors in an attempt to evade their pursuers. The sound of hobnailed boots and gunshots echoed through the corridors of the hospital. The two Volunteers stopped occasionally at corners and fired their rifles to slow down their pursuers. These encounters developed into a deadly game of hide and seek. As they reached the front of the building the Volunteers threw themselves through the ground floor windows, out onto the lawn. As he staggered to regain his footing, Dan McCarthy was shot and wounded in the stomach. He shouted, 'Run on! I'm hit.'[12]

Jim Kenny lay face down on the grass momentarily, his weapon trained on the area where he expected the British to appear. The first soldier to appear beat a hasty retreat and Kenny sprinted across to the main buildings, only to find his escape route blocked by another platoon of soldiers. Kenny levelled his rifle and opened fire on the soldiers, forcing them to retreat into a nearby building. As he ran, bullets hit the brickwork behind him sending showers of masonry into the air. He ran past the convent and as he reached the Protestant infirmary he found Commandant Ceannt who was assisting a wounded Volunteer. Ceannt had been reconnoitring his positions when he found himself cut off by the rapid advance of the Royal Irish Regiment. In order to evade the British troops it was decided to leave their wounded comrade until they could find a secure means of escape. Accidentally they entered a cul de sac (13) between the Protestant Hospital and the Catholic Women's Hospital. Both men prepared for a sudden rush of soldiers and a desperate fight to the end, but no one appeared in the alleyway. They were attempting to force open a wooden gate at the end of the alleyway when suddenly a patient appeared at a window above them and offered them a ladder to scale the wall of the Protestant Hospital. Kenny climbed up first and on reaching the top, trained his rifle on the corner of the alley in order to cover Ceannt's assent. The commandant followed and on entering the Protestant Hospital he requested that the matron assist the Volunteer who was wounded outside. Assisted by two patients, the matron brought the wounded man indoors. Ceannt then consulted his map and planned the best route back to his headquarters. By chance a nun opened a gateway nearby, offering an escape route via the rear of the Catholic Women's Hospital. Both Ceannt and Kenny returned safely to headquarters.[13]

Having cleared the ground floor of Hospital 2–3 of Volunteers, the British troops were momentarily pinned down by rifle fire from the upper floor. The six Volunteers fired furiously into the approaching ranks. They then vacated their position and retreated towards the west wing of the building along an endless warren of intersecting corridors. As the British prepared to assault the upper floor, there was a sudden lull in the firing. Two nurses had taken cover on the second floor of Hospital 2–3 and as the noise subsided, one of them, Margaret Keogh, believing that the fighting had ceased, started down the stairs. At the foot of the stairway, a door leading to a porch opened off the long corridor. Two British soldiers had taken up position there, covering the stairway. As Nurse Keogh reached the bottom step and appeared in the doorway she was shot dead. Her friend screamed at the soldiers to stop. An officer appeared and shouted to her: 'Are there any Sinn Féiners upstairs?' The nurse pleaded with the soldiers to place her friend's body on a table, which they did. Nurse Margaret Keogh came from Leighlinbridge, Carlow, and was the daughter of Patrick Blanchfield Keogh, the coroner for County Carlow.

As this episode was unfolding, wounded Volunteer Dan McCarthy was carried into the hospital by a patient and laid beside the body of Nurse Keogh. McCarthy was bleeding profusely from his stomach wound and was removed to a medical ward in the Union by British soldiers and Union staff. He hid his revolver under his pillow. The British entered the ward and came over to his bed. They threatened to kill the wounded Volunteer by running him through with a bayonet, but an officer intervened and said: 'Stop that.' With that one of the other patients in the ward shouted: 'He has just put a gun under his pillow.' The officer then took charge of the revolver and McCarthy was removed to another ward and kept under guard.[14]

At Hospital 2–3 (5) the British troops climbed the stairs to the second floor and began searching for the six Volunteers who had fired on them earlier. Using a pass key the soldiers entered the west wing and found that a partition door separated them from their quarry. They shouted to the Volunteers to surrender and, using the key to gain entry, they charged through the door in force. The area was so narrow that both sides were unable to fire and a fierce hand-to-hand struggle ensued. Despite fighting desperately, the hopelessly outnumbered Volunteers were forced to surrender and were led out of the Union complex to captivity.[15]

Outside Hospital 2–3, over the wide spaces of the South Dublin Union and through the many buildings, a bloody game of hide and seek was taking place. Having advanced deep into the Union, the British troops now turned their attention to the Catholic Women's Hospital (11). After surviving the killing fields of McCaffrey's Estate, Volunteer Section Commander John Joyce and the surviving members of his unit were resting briefly in the corridors of the Women's Hospital. It was just past 5 p.m. when the British military launched their attack on that building. As they broke through the locked doors, the soldiers could hear the screams and shrieks of the female patients who had not been evacuated by the Union officials. The soldiers proceeded with great caution into the maze of corridors.

The Volunteers had heard the British troops entering and had taken up firing positions, lying prone on the floor at the intersection of wards sixteen and seventeen. Later Joyce remembered the smell of the waxed floors filling his senses. His plan was to catch the approaching enemy in a confined area and inflict heavy casualties thus forcing them to retire. It was a desperate plan. The patients had taken cover in a corner of the dormitory, protected by upturned beds and mattresses. British soldiers appeared at the doorway and Joyce was the first to open fire. The patients screamed as rifle fire reverberated through the ward. Joyce jumped to his feet and slammed the door of the ward shut. Smoke and the smell of cordite filled the room. He heard the British soldiers shouting, 'Surrender in the name of the King'. Joyce and his men took cover as British troops opened fire. The Volunteers were adamant they were not going to surrender.

The firing suddenly stopped. An educated English voice demanded, 'I will count to five. Either surrender or we are coming in.'[16]

The Volunteers listened intently to the count: 'One, two, three ...' They did not wait for the final numbers. Jumping to their feet they dashed through the ward and down the corridor, the end of which was barred by a locked door. Without stopping, Joyce fired and blew the lock off, kicked the door open and continued to run on into the next ward. Throwing themselves on the floor the Volunteers turned and took aim at their pursuers. Shots echoed through the ward as each side desperately tried to kill the other. Screams and smoke filled the room as a number of the British soldiers were wounded. The Volunteers fought a desperate rearguard action in their attempts to escape from the warren of corridors in the Women's Hospital. Joyce remembered running through deserted wards and empty corridors, the noise and vibrations of the battle fading behind him. Once outside, he felt the evening air on his face and before him he saw headquarters, the Nurses' Home (10). Joyce and his section had evaded capture.[17]

Chapter 4

Easter Monday, 24 April 1916
Evening

Just before dusk, Vice-Commandant Cathal Brugha called for two Volunteers for a special duty. William McDowell, a recent recruit to the Volunteer movement, and James Coughlan came forward. Their mission was to enter McCaffrey's Estate through the door at the rear of the Nurses' Home (10) and bring in some wounded Volunteers. It was a dangerous mission as the area of the estate and headquarters was under constant fire from British soldiers positioned in the Royal Hospital.

Taking two Union patients with them, McDowell and Coughlan dashed through the door out into the open field. As they ran for cover, the Volunteers saw some of their number taking cover thirty yards to their right. Crossing a barbed wire entanglement they joined their comrades. Coughlan enquired as to the exact location of the enemy and was told they were directly in front of the hiding place. The British fire was so intense that bullets became embedded a few inches above ground level in the large wall behind their position. British troops who had entered via the Rialto gate had concealed themselves in hedging just fifty yards to the front of the Volunteers' position. There was very little cover for the Volunteers except for a fold in the ground. Machine-gun fire from the Royal Hospital was also enfilading their position.

Pinned down and unable to return fire, the Volunteers remained in this predicament for some time. Coughlan shouted to McDowell to keep his head down as bullets kicked up the earth around them. The position was hopeless and Coughlan received orders down the line that he was to return to the Nurses' Home and cover the withdrawal of the Volunteers from McCaffrey's Estate from that position. In full view of the enemy, Coughlan ran the gauntlet back to the wall, negotiating the barbed wire fence as gunfire cracked from the bushes. Covering the entrance with his rifle, Coughlan waited for his comrades. After what seemed like an eternity, Volunteers began to pass through the doorway. Captain Seán McGlynn appeared and ordered Coughlan to barricade the door. However, Coughlan protested, as he had not seen McDowell come through.

In McCaffrey's Estate, McDowell had attempted to lay down a covering fire as the Volunteers withdrew from their position. Unknown to him, a force of British soldiers had attacked and taken Hospital 2–3 (5), which overlooked the field. As McDowell withdrew from his position, he was shot and killed by a British soldier on the second floor of the hospital. William McDowell was forty-four years old and an enthusiastic member of the Gaelic League. A painter by trade, he lived at No. 10 Merchants Quay in Dublin city. He left behind a widow and four children. His brother was also a Volunteer and was in action at the Four Courts. Eventually, Coughlan reluctantly accepted Captain McGlynn's order and barricaded the door. The dead and the wounded lay where they had fallen.[18]

Commandant Ceannt sent a female hospital official from the South Dublin Union to the British military with a written message requesting a short ceasefire in order to remove the wounded and to bury the dead.

'We shall give you no terms, you have killed our Major' (meaning Ramsay) was their reply. The officer then tore up the note. When the news that a British officer was dead was reported to Ceannt, the Volunteers cheered.[19] The firing continued.

Ceannt's men at the main gate of the Union (14) had been under continuous fire from the machine-gun position at the Royal Hospital since early afternoon. As darkness spread throughout the complex, the hours of intense fighting began to take their toll on the Volunteers. Max Caulfield describes the day of warfare:

> The fighting had deteriorated into a game of cat and mouse; a nerve-racking, heart-stopping battle of unexpected death, with rarely a let up. A sense of purpose, a flame of patriotism, still flickered strongly, but by now abstract conceptions had given way to realities and battle had been pared down to its true components. The pressure, in short, had begun to tell.[20]

It is estimated that forty-eight men, twenty-five of whom were stationed at headquarters at the Nurses' Home, were defending the area inside the front of James's Street. The buildings dominated the inside courtyard giving the defenders maximum cover as well as a clear field of fire over the South Dublin Union. A sentry in the Nurses' Home became convinced that the British were digging a trench in McCaffrey's Estate that would allow them to breach the Union's defences. He woke Lieutenant Cosgrave, who withdrew his pistol from his holster and cautiously moved out into the night. On investigation Cosgrave realised that the trench the sentry was seeing was in fact a pathway of a small house, so he returned to his post to reassure the sentry. However, the sentry then stated that he could hear digging. Cosgrave could also hear a noise, but on investigation he found a loose window blind flapping in the evening breeze. Many of the troops were suffering from nervous exhaustion and nerves were very taut.

By nightfall, the shooting had almost ceased except for sporadic sniper fire. Brugha organised a group of Volunteers to counteract the British fire. He ordered them to return fire at the plumes of smoke from the British snipers' positions. Firing soon ceased entirely and an uneasy silence descended on the Union. The Volunteers received their first respite of the day, a meal of corned beef and tea. Their morale remained high as Ceannt toured the positions and encouraged his men. He praised them for their actions under trying conditions and stated that a GHQ had been established in the General Post Office on Sackville Street. Later, at the Nurses' Home, Ceannt and Brugha inspected survey maps by torchlight. Brugha detailed guards for the night and the men knelt and recited a decade of the rosary before retiring. Not many slept.

Peadar Doyle and another Volunteer took up guard duty in a room facing the square. As they prepared their post, a cartridge jammed in one of their Howth Mauser rifles causing it to accidentally discharge with a loud bang that alarmed the camp. However, calm was soon restored.

In the day's fighting at the Union, both the Volunteers and the British military had suffered heavy casualties. Commandant Ceannt had also lost many of his posts within the Union, but had consolidated his position in the north of the complex.

On the British side the regimental history of the Royal Irish Regiment states: 'The young soldiers of the battalion behaved in a splendid manner despite the trying conditions, and although to many it was their first experience of warfare.'[21] Having driven the Volunteers back from their outlying posts, the British crown forces now occupied most of the Union.

The first British reinforcements began to reach Dublin city as the battle in the South Dublin Union raged. Colonel Portal arrived at Kingsbridge Station with the advance guard of the Curragh Mobile Column, from County Kildare. Portal's 3rd Reserve Cavalry Brigade consisted of 1,500 armed troops, made up of soldiers from the 8th Reserve Cavalry Regiment (16th/17th Lancers, King Edward's Horse, Dorsetshire, Oxfordshire Yeomanry); 9th Reserve Cavalry Regiment (3rd/7th Hussars, 2nd/3rd County of London Yeomanry); and 10th Reserve Cavalry Regiment (4th/8th Hussars, Lancashire Hussars, Duke of Lancasters/Westmorland/Cumberland Yeomanry). Having assessed the situation, Portal sent a third of his force by the loop railway line to the North Wall. He then set off to

Dublin Castle with the remainder of his troops. The Irish Volunteers had failed to seal off a number of access routes to Dublin Castle and Colonel Portal moved his force in without meeting any serious opposition. The khaki noose was beginning to tighten.

Chapter 5

Tuesday 25 and
Wednesday 26 April 1916

At 3.45 a.m. on Tuesday, Brigadier General W.H.M. Lowe arrived at Kingsbridge Station with the 25th Infantry Reserve Brigade from the Curragh army camp in County Kildare. Upon his arrival Lowe took personal command of British crown forces in Dublin city. A veteran soldier, Brigadier General Lowe joined the army in 1881 serving in the Egyptian campaign of 1882 and the Burma expedition of 1886. During the Boer War in 1901, Lowe was promoted to the rank of lieutenant colonel and his offensive tactics during this conflict brought him to the attention of his superiors. By 1916 Brigadier General Lowe was the officer commanding the 3rd Reserve Cavalry Brigade, a training component located at the Curragh army camp in County Kildare. The force consisted of the 5th Battalion (extra reserve) Royal Dublin Fusiliers and the 5th Battalion (extra reserve), the Prince of Wales Leinster Regiment. The addition of Lowe's troops brought the total of British military forces in Dublin to 4,650 men.

In England, Major General A.E. Sandbach, CB, DSO, received orders to mobilise the 59th North Midland Division and move immediately to Ireland. This division consisted of three brigades: the 176th (2/5th, 2/6th, South Staffordshire Regiment, 2/5th, 2/6th North Staffordshire Regiment); 177th (2/4th, 2/5th Lincolnshire Regiment, 2/4th, 2/5th Leicestershire Regiment); and 178th (2/5th, 2/6th, 2/7th and 2/8th battalions of the Sherwood Forester Regiment). The first components of the North Midland Division would begin to arrive in Ireland by Tuesday evening.[22]

At 5.30 a.m. on Tuesday a barrage of rifle fire lasting ten minutes was opened up on the Volunteers' positions in the Union. Section Commander of 'C' Company, Frank (Gobbon) Burke moved through the Nurses' Home as Volunteers stood to their posts. He took up position beside Volunteer Fogarty who had just lit his pipe. As Burke leaned over to light his cigarette from Fogarty's match, a shot rang out. A bullet came through the front window of the building, hitting Burke in the throat. Only moments before, Burke had warned his section to keep their heads down. As he slowly expired, his colleagues knelt and prayed by his side. Lieutenant Alfie Byrne entered the room and berated Fogarty stating, 'You are responsible for that man's death.' Fogarty was so guilt-ridden by the accusation that he lost his mind and had to be disarmed and put under the care of another Volunteer. Fogarty remained in this deranged state for many weeks.[23]

Frank Burke was the brother of Joan Burke, the Irish contralto, and also the stepbrother of Lieutenant Cosgrave, who had got him involved in the Volunteers. Devastated at the loss, Cosgrave described Burke as, 'one of the best Volunteers in the battalion, energetic, untiring and devoted to his comrades with whom he was most popular'. Cosgrave carried the guilt of involving his stepbrother in the Irish Volunteers for the rest of his life.[24]

From an upper window of the Nurses' Home Volunteer James Foran hoisted an improvised flag, an emerald harp, painted on a window blind. As the flag was raised the Volunteers stood to attention and sang 'A Nation Once Again'. From their hard-won positions, the British crown forces could clearly see the flag flapping in the breeze. British positions opened fire. Fusillade after fusillade was directed at the flagpole. The fire was so intense that a number of stray shots killed some civilians. Mrs Heffernan, who lived in a large tenement building on James's Street called the Crimea House (so named because this is where shirts were produced for soldiers heading to fight at Balaclava in the 1850s), was killed in her room, and a visitor from Belfast, Mr Halliday, was shot dead as he walked along the South Circular Road. Yet still the British military failed to bring down the flag.

Inside the Union, the Volunteers worked tirelessly while their flag was being fired on. Brugha ordered that everything capable of holding water was to be filled in case the supply should be cut off and to safeguard against fire. Moreover, all foodstuffs were collected and handed over to Volunteer quartermaster, Peadar Doyle. The Volunteers located in the boardroom over the main entrance of the Union (14), completed their task of tunnelling through the walls, thus linking the main entrance structure with that of the rear yard of the Nurses' Home.

At headquarters, Commandant Ceannt directed that the front door of the Nurses' Home be reinforced. Once the main door was secure, boards were nailed across the porch doors. Two barricades were then erected to form a second line of defence a couple of yards behind the front entrance. The barricades were about five and seven feet high, one towering over the other, the hoardings of planks about a foot apart, and the space in between packed tightly with clay and rubble. Clothing belonging to the nurses was filled with clay and used to reinforce the windows. The building had become a fortress.

Local priests, Father Dillon and Father Gerhard, OCC, spent an hour visiting the Volunteers, hearing their confessions. Morale among the Volunteers remained high as supporters threw food parcels and personal messages over the wall. The Volunteers also had assistance from an unusual source: three officials of the Union, William Murphy, Patrick Smyth and Laurence Tallon were sympathisers of the republican cause and assisted the Volunteers during the week. Two of the men provided Ceannt with information and delivered messages, while William Murphy, a storekeeper clerk, took food supplies by horse and cart to the various departments. Accompanied by a young lady, Murphy used a white flag tied to a broom handle in order to distinguish himself from the warring factions. Ceannt asked for supplies of corned beef or bacon, but Murphy could only offer items such as tea, sugar and condensed milk, which were gratefully received by the Volunteers.[25] The crown forces also demanded food, which the storekeeper supplied. The bakeries within the Union were manned throughout the week, supplying not only those within the Union but also the people in the local area with loaves of bread. Local priests braved the gunfire to bring assistance to their parishioners.

Returning from a day trip to Belfast on Monday, Assistant Matron of the South Dublin Union Annie Mannion found she could not gain entry to the complex. Although the main entrance was barricaded, she finally managed to gain access through the Rialto gate early on Tuesday morning. The Union was under constant fire as the matron made her way to her residence beside the mortuary (17). Donning her uniform she proceeded to the food stores, planning to give provisions to the mental patients in the wards nearby. Being careful not to be caught in the crossfire, she and a few others loaded supplies onto a horse and cart and, under a Red Cross flag, began deliveries around the Union. According to Miss Mannion, British crown forces had not taken up any permanent positions within the Union and continued to move from building to building. Casualties of the fighting were cared for in the hospital and Miss Mannion stated that those patients who died during the week were buried in temporary graves in the grounds until the hostilities ceased. British casualties were removed by ambulance.[26]

By Tuesday evening, British military forces had withdrawn from their positions within the South Dublin Union. Having almost taken the complex, the Royal Irish Regiment was unhappy with the order to withdraw. Their regimental history states:

The battalion, under orders from headquarters, remained in occupation of the Union for the night (Monday) and on the following morning, for some extraordinary reason, it was directed to evacuate the Union and concentrate at Kingsbridge Station. This was done under protest.[27]

The majority of the regiment moved to Kingsbridge Station to await further orders.

Colonel Portal's troops from the Curragh mobile column had established a line of posts from Kingsbridge Station to Trinity College via Dublin Castle by noon on Tuesday 25 April. This manoeuvre divided the Volunteer forces in two, giving a safe line of advance for British troops who now began to extend operations to the north and south.

In order to secure the area near Ceannt's position, crown forces occupied Number 98 James's Street, a building owned by the Guinness Brewery. From this post they were able to survey the local area. British soldiers positioned at the Royal Hospital and surrounding areas continued to keep up a steady rate of machine-gun and sniper fire into the Union grounds. Cathal Brugha and a couple of Volunteers continued to answer the sniper fire from the Royal Hospital and towards evening the British ceased fire.

At 8 p.m. on Tuesday evening, Ceannt and Brugha sent Volunteers Seán Murphy and Liam O'Flaherty to try to make contact with Captain Tom McCarthy's section at the outpost established at Roe's Distillery. Under the cover of darkness, the two men left the Union through a small wicket gate near the rear of the Nurses' Home and dashed out onto James's Street. Avoiding military patrols, they travelled up and down Mount Brown and Cromwell's Quarters, trying to locate Captain McCarthy's men. To their surprise they discovered that the post had been vacated leaving the flank of the Union exposed. The caretaker of the distillery stated that the Volunteers had vacated the position because they had no provisions and were unable to hold the building.[28] Captain McCarthy had made the fatal error of withdrawing from his position instead of reinforcing the garrison in the Union.

Another of Ceannt's outposts was stationed at Watkins' Brewery at Ardee Street under the command of Con Colbert, who regarded this position as somewhat ineffective. Unable to make contact with Ceannt, Colbert sent for instructions to Major John MacBride who was stationed at Jacob's biscuit factory on Aungier Street. The Major directed him to reinforce the Volunteer garrison at the outpost in the Marrowbone Lane Distillery. At 6 p.m. on Wednesday evening, Colbert moved his force under the cover of darkness to support those at Marrowbone

Lane. With the addition of Colbert's section, the garrison increased to over 100 Volunteers, with forty women of Cumann na mBan among its ranks. That afternoon at the Marrowbone Lane Distillery there had been a serious battle between Volunteers and British crown forces. Robert Holland and his colleagues within the distillery stopped a British attempt to storm the building. The crown forces suffered serious losses; their dead and wounded were strewn along the canal bank and the surrounds of the building.

Throughout the afternoon, however, British sniper fire increased in intensity and accuracy and Volunteer Mick Liston received a serious wound to the head. The continuous fire from the British positions surrounding the distillery forced Holland to evacuate his firing position temporarily. Later he resumed his post and attempted to counteract the British sniper fire. On the previous day Holland had noticed what he thought was a woman leaning from a window at a nearby house, an act he thought reckless due to the gunfire in the area. Holland remarked:

She had a hat, blouse and apron on her and I got suspicious. I told Mick Callaghan that I was going to have a shot at her. He said, 'No.' I said it was a queer place for a woman to be and that it was queer she should have a hat on her, as she must have seen the bullets flying around but took no notice of them. I made up my mind. She was only thirty-five or forty yards away from me and I fired at her. She sagged halfway out of the window. The hat and small little shawl fell off her and I saw what I took to be a woman was a man in shirt sleeves.[29]

Throughout Wednesday, British sniper fire continued as Volunteers Holland and a bandaged Mick Liston returned fire from their concealed positions in the distillery. Liston fired at a British soldier sitting on the branch of a tree 200 yards from his position. The figure of the British soldier jerked as he was hit – his lifeless body slumped forward and hung from the tree for the remainder of the day. The Volunteers noticed that a group of enemy soldiers had taken up firing positions behind a number of tree stumps. Having fired a volley at the distillery, one soldier left cover and was promptly shot dead by Liston. The others, numbering about a dozen, broke cover and retreated along the canal bank. The Volunteers fired rapidly into the ranks of the retreating soldiers hitting all of them. Some collapsed and others staggered back towards the bridge at Rialto.

By 5.30 a.m. on Wednesday, British troops of the 59th North Midland Division disembarked at Kingstown harbour (Dún Laoghaire). While some of the division remained in reserve, the 178th Infantry Brigade (comprising the 2/7th and 2/8th battalions of the Sherwood Forester Regiment) under the command of Brigadier Colonel Maconchy followed the coast road through Ballsbridge towards Trinity College.

During Easter week there were a number of Irish Volunteers who attempted to link up with their respective units. Although Eoin MacNeill's countermanding order of the previous Sunday had caused many men not to turn out initially, as the week progressed a number of Volunteers came out of their own accord. Due to the cordon of British troops around the city, these Volunteers were unable to join their units. However, they were undeterred and began harassing crown forces by taking up sniping positions, injuring many and delaying the British advance into the city.

By nightfall, both battalions of the Sherwood Foresters had suffered heavy casualties having engaged Irish Volunteer forces on Northumberland Road and at Mount Street Bridge. Relieved by the South Staffordshire Regiment, the remnants of the Sherwood Foresters made their way to the Royal Dublin Society where they billeted overnight.

On Wednesday evening, as the battle raged throughout Dublin city, the Volunteers in the South Dublin Union could move freely around the inner courtyard since the

British military had ceased firing and had withdrawn their forces from within the complex. However, although the Volunteers did not know it, this was just the calm before the storm.

Chapter 6

Thursday, 27 April 1916 Morning

During the night of 26–27 April, the Sherwood Forester Regiment received orders from Brigadier General Lowe to concentrate their forces in the Royal Hospital, Kilmainham.[30] They were detailed to escort a consignment of ammunition to the headquarters' building. Lieutenant Colonel Oates would lead the advance guard that consisted of the 2/8th Sherwood Foresters, who would then be followed by the main body of the regiment comprising the 2/7th Sherwood Foresters, Brigade Headquarters, the Royal Engineers and the Army Service Corps. The 2/7th Sherwood Foresters would also throw out a small rearguard.

The convoy was to follow a route that crossed Leeson

Street Bridge, went past Wellington barracks (now Griffith College), and continued along the South Circular Road, across Rialto Bridge and on to the Royal Hospital, Kilmainham. Lieutenant Colonel Oates was familiar with the route, as he had been stationed at Wellington barracks for two years when he had served with the Munster Fusiliers.

On the previous day, Wednesday 26 April, the 2/5th and 2/6th Sherwood Foresters had crossed the Rialto Bridge without incident. British crown forces expected little or no opposition on the journey. Ammunition was issued to the men while the Army Service Corps loaded the wagons. Accompanying Lieutenant Colonel Oates were two veterans of the First World War, Captain 'Mickey' Martyn and Lieutenant Colonel Oates' son, Captain John S. Oates, the officer commanding 'D' company. Captain Martyn had fought on the Western Front in actions at 'Plug Street' and Neuve Chapelle. Both of these officers had missed the action at Mount Street Bridge, as 'D' company of the 2/8th Sherwood Foresters had been held up in Liverpool. They now joined the somewhat depleted ranks of the other companies of the Sherwood Foresters and prepared to move out.

Thursday morning broke as a calm and beautiful spring morning. From their vantage points within the Union complex, the Volunteers could see people moving freely through the surrounding streets, stopping to chat and going about their daily business. Having procured razors many men took the opportunity to wash and shave. The atmosphere was relaxed as the Volunteers stretched their legs in the small garden to the rear of the Nurses' Home. Brugha, seated on the floor of that building, dismantled and cleaned his automatic pistol. He carefully reloaded his empty clips. Commandant Ceannt arrived and the two officers assessed the situation. Their entire force now consisted of only forty-one officers and men, as eight of the Volunteers had been killed in action and another twelve were either wounded or taken prisoner. They held the boardroom and the offices over the main entrance as well as the Nurses' Home (10). Their positions covered James's Street on the outside and from the inside, the main courtyard as well as the fields between the Rialto entrance and the main gate. They had lost all contact with their outlying posts.

A dispatch had been received from Volunteer headquarters at the General Post Office that morning. The news was positive, but the messenger reported that he had great difficulty in breaking through the British lines in order to deliver the communiqué. Commandant Ceannt decided not to send a written reply but relayed verbally the events of the previous days to the messenger. The Volunteers watched him leave and wondered if the message would make it to Patrick Pearse and the headquarter staff.

By this stage the hospital staff had transferred many of the patients in the wards adjoining Ceannt's positions to the Rialto end of the complex for their safety. Ceannt was anticipating an all out attack on the Union in the near future and instructed his men to make ready. Ammunition was distributed to each section of Volunteers and Ceannt and Brugha toured the defences encouraging their men. Both Volunteer officers were confident of their position in the Union. They claimed that though setbacks were possible, the Volunteers would not be defeated. The sentiment among the Volunteers was that this was a fight of the spirit, for the spirit is never conquered. In the hours that were to follow, this belief would be put to the test.

Chapter 7

Thursday, 27 April 1916
Early Afternoon

In the early afternoon, the British column heading for the Royal Hospital, Kilmainham, accompanied by Brigadier General Maconchy, set off from the Ballsbridge Showgrounds. As they approached Rialto Street at 2.15 p.m., a fusillade was opened on the column causing a number of horses to stampede. The advance guard of the column led by Lieutenant Colonel Oates took cover on the approach to Rialto Bridge. Irish Volunteers had opened fire in an attempt to delay the column's advance.

Lieutenant Colonel Oates ordered Captain Martyn to take a section from the leading company and clear the buildings in Rialto, and also those in the vicinity of the bridge, of rogue snipers. As Captain Martyn moved to counteract the sniping, a number of shots came from a nearby rhubarb field, south-west of Rialto Bridge. Soldiers scattered as more shots also came from the buildings of the South Dublin Union. The military were forced to take cover as single shots snapped through the nearby trees that ran parallel to the road.

Brigadier General Maconchy took the decision to risk sending one wagon across the bridge. The army service driver approached the bridge at a gallop and a volley of shots rang out, many of them hitting the wooded slats of the wagon. Although the vehicle cleared the bridge, Brigadier Maconchy realised he would suffer severe casualties if he attempted to get the rest of the transport across. The approach to Rialto Bridge was a steep and narrow defile that would slow the column and make it an easy target for Irish snipers. The column was halted and Lieutenant Colonel Oates realised that he had to thoroughly clear the way ahead and protect the column's flanks in order to proceed safely. Captain Dimock, leading 'A' company, was ordered to clear the rhubarb field, then cross the bridge and clear out the enemy snipers ahead of the main advance. 'C' company were brought up to secure the line of advance along the South Circular Road. Lieutenant Colonel Oates sent an urgent message to Portobello barracks requesting re-inforcements.

Sir Francis Fletcher Vane of the Royal Munster Fusiliers responded to Oates' request for assistance. Vane assembled all the men not on duty, about fifty in all, many of them from the Royal Irish Rifles, with no fewer than six officers from five different regiments.[31] Two members of the Royal Irish Constabulary, Constable Christopher Miller and Constable Martin Meany accompanied the soldiers. They were conspicuous in their uniforms as they wore army khaki breeches and the police cap and tunic. Both men were attending the school of instruction for non-commissioned officers at the barracks. They marched out of the barracks and found the convoy in great trouble about two miles away. The men were already suffering from battle fatigue after their engagement at Mount Street Bridge the day before and Lieutenant Colonel Oates was greatly distracted.

Captain Martyn returned to the column having completed his task and received further orders from Oates:

The advance guard to clear the Auxiliary Workhouse (3), and occupy as much as possible of the South Dublin Union, with a view to distracting the enemy's attention whilst the transport crossed the bridge.[32]

Lieutenant Colonel Oates handed over command of the

assault on the Union to Sir Francis Fletcher Vane. Major Vane wore a soft peaked cap and carried a swagger stick that he used to direct his men to their positions. As the troops made ready, the column made contact with Lieutenant Monk Gibbon who was newly arrived from Kingsbridge Station with a number of men. As the lieutenant's unit approached the bridge from the station direction they came under fire from a section of the Sherwood Foresters. As his men took cover, the lieutenant called out and the firing ceased. By mistakenly firing on their own soldiers the British troops showed that they were nervous and suffering from exhaustion. Approaching the column, Gibbon offered his services to Major Vane who was glad to have more experienced troops under his command. Vane directed the men to where he could see a rebel flag flying from the rooftop. That was to be their target. Entering the Union grounds, British soldiers moved north, spreading out in a skirmish line across the open ground. Advancing in short runs, about five sections of twenty men each moved towards the Nurses' Home.

Major Vane and Captain Martyn led the first wave that moved swiftly through the Auxiliary Workhouse (3) at the Rialto end, which they found unoccupied. In close support were Captain Oates and another section advancing in a series of rushes. Wave after wave of soldiers advanced through the Union gaining seven to eight yards in each advancing movement. As each section took up position they concentrated their fire on the windows of the buildings occupied by the Volunteers, enabling the other sections to move forward. Major Vane described the assault in a letter to his wife:

> Well I have been in some fights but never in such an odd one as this, for we commenced by open fighting in fields and so far as right flank was concerned fought up to literally three feet of the enemy. But everything was bizarre on that day for we advanced through a convent where the nuns were all praying and expecting to be shot poor creatures, then through the wards of imbeciles who were all shrieking – and through one of poor old people. To get from one door to another was a gymnastic feat because you had to run the gauntlet of the snipers.[33]

Having passed through the chapel in the convent (8), the soldiers had 250 yards of open ground to negotiate. Lieutenant Gibbon and his unit remained in support, lying on the grass to the rear. When the advance troop reached an outcrop of buildings, they summoned the support group. Dashing through the grounds, Lieutenant Gibbon made his way into a small orchard near the rear of the Nurses' Home. Volunteer sentries were the first to open fire on the khaki figures as the shout of 'alarm, stand to' was given by the Volunteer lookouts. As Gibbon's men took cover, the air was filled with shattering noise and confusion. Men shouted to one another, gunfire rattled out from the buildings and explosions cracked throughout the complex. Lance Corporal Chapman, gamekeeper to the Duke of Newcastle, was shot and killed as he advanced towards the Volunteers' position.

A number of the Volunteer garrison had been engaged in wall-boring operations in the buildings between the front offices over the main gate at James's Street (14) and the Nurses' Home (10). When this was completed, the pierced walls enabled the Volunteers to move freely from the offices to headquarters at the Nurses' Home. When they heard the shooting, they grabbed their rifles and rushed to their positions in the Nurses' Home. A well-directed and concentrated fire was being maintained against all the windows to the rear of the building by the British. Many of the bullets entered the rooms diagonally, splitting the brickwork at the sides of the windows, preventing the Volunteers from returning fire. The machine-gunners on the roof of the Royal Hospital added to the intense fire that was now being directed into the Union complex.

The gunfire was so intense that the rooms in the Nurses' Home soon filled with dense clouds of plaster dust. Bullets flew through the back windows, entered the rooms and exited through the front of the building. The Volunteers crouched low behind the granite walls of the building for cover. Volunteer James Coughlan, unable to return fire, moved out from the rear room to the first landing that overlooked the front entrance of the Nurses' Home. Looking over the porch barricade, his field of fire covered the windows at the side of the front door. Taking cover behind a sand-bagged emplacement on the landing, he was joined by Douglas fFrench Mullen and Jack Doherty. Khaki figures darted across the front of the building and the Volunteers opened a rapid fire.

Some British soldiers entered the wards (11) that were opposite the Nurses' Home. The ward staff incorrectly reported that the Irish Volunteers numbered in the region of 200 men. After breaking the windows, the British soldiers opened fire in an attempt to cover a frontal assault on the Volunteer headquarters. The frontage of the Nurses' Home was raked by a terrible concentration of rifle fire. A party of soldiers broke cover and charged across the square towards the Nurses' Home. They were repulsed and retreated suffering heavy casualties, one of whom, Constable Meany, was severely wounded. This scenario was repeated a number of times.

Volunteer Peadar Doyle noticed that the barricade at the front door had been tampered with and reported this to Commandant Ceannt. Both men made a desperate dash to the entrance. As they put their shoulders to the now open door in an attempt to close it, they felt a huge force pushing from the other side. Constable Miller of the Royal Irish Constabulary had seen the door open and was now forcing his way in. Constable Christopher Miller was thirty years old and originally from County Limerick. He had eight years and three months of service with the RIC. As he heaved on the door Ceannt and Doyle slid across the floor as they lost their footing. The RIC man was almost six foot tall and of a strong build. He was gaining the upper hand and the door was slowly opening. Then Ceannt stuck his automatic pistol out through the gap in the door and squeezed the trigger. The policeman was hit and he staggered backwards a few yards before collapsing. The Volunteers managed to close the door and secure the position.[34] Lieutenant Monk Gibbon was called upon to give aid to the stricken policeman. He picked up a water bottle and darted across in front of the Volunteers' position, but as soon as he reached Miller's body he could see by his pallor that he was dead.

Cathal Brugha, from his vantage point at the window on the first floor of the Nurses' Home, directed fire into the advancing British troops. From their vantage point overlooking a warren of side streets, alleyways, windows and rooftops, the Volunteers fired on any soldier who moved into range.

A squad of eight British soldiers moved across the square reaching the Bakehouse (18) between the Nurses' Home and the Boardroom (14). One soldier was shot dead as he entered the building and another was severely wounded. Leaving two men to hold that position and provide covering fire, the remaining four crept out into a courtyard that flanked the Nurses' Home. They gained cover by moving along the wall of the yard until they came to a barred window that was eight feet from the ground. Removing the pin from a hand grenade they dropped it through the window into the dormitory building that was adjacent to the Nurses' Home. Unknown to the soldiers a number of patients had taken refuge from the fighting there and as the missile exploded one Union patient was killed and eight others were wounded.

Major Vane soon realised that a frontal assault on the Nurses' Home was hopeless, as the building had been well barricaded. He ordered Captain Martyn to outflank the defenders by entering the long series of buildings (9) to the left of the Volunteer headquarters. This building housed a number of wards for the elderly. Entering the cold stone building he led his section into a labyrinth of corridors until they reached the dividing wall between the buildings. They were separated from the Nurses' Home by a brick wall nine inches thick. Captain Martyn sent some of his men for tools to breach the wall and they

Commandant
Éamonn Ceannt

Vice-Commandant
Cathal Brugha
(Kilmainham Gaol Archives)

Lieutenant William Cosgrave
(Kilmainham Gaol Archives)

The main entrance of the South Dublin Union (Professor Coakley)

Rear of the main entrance (D119/29, Military Archives)

View of the Royal Hospital, Kilmainham, from the South Dublin Union (D119/9, Military Archives)

The Nurses' Home, 4th Battalion's Headquarters in the South Dublin Union (Professor Coakley)

Volunteer Robert Holland's position (in the tower) in Marrowbone
Lane Distillery (D125/11, Military Archives)

Survivors of the South Dublin Union garrison in the 1960s
(Maureen Burke)

The hall and staircase in the Nurses' Home where Brugha held off repeated attacks by the British (D119/19, Military Archives)

Captain John Oates
(Sherwood Forester Museum)

Captain 'Micky' Martyn
(Sherwood Forester Museum)

Lewis machine-
gun detachment
(Sherwood Forester
Museum)

Sir Francis Fletcher Vane
(Professor Coakley)

Lieutenant Colonel Oates on the right (Sherwood Forester Museum)

The grave of Constable Christopher Miller, RIC, in the grounds of the Royal Hospital Kilmainham (Author's collection)

Sergeants of the Sherwood Foresters *c.*1915
(Sherwood Forester Museum)

Soldiers of the 2/7th and 2/8th Sherwood Foresters resting after
their engagement on Mount Street during the 1916 Easter Rising
(de Valera Papers, University College Dublin)

returned with a small coal pick (an implement with a hammer at one end and pick at the other). The wall was soon breached and two soldiers began crawling through the narrow entrance. This action went unnoticed due to the din of battle.

From their vantage point on the landing within the Nurses' Home, the Volunteers saw a khaki cap appear through the hole in the wall. Jack Doherty opened fire and the British soldier slumped as he was hit. The other Volunteers opened fire, the intensity of their actions causing their rifles to overheat. Spent cartridges littered the floor.

James Coughlan discarded his rifle and emptied the contents of his Webley revolver into the barricade. He shouted to fFrench Mullen to throw a grenade. The captain lit the fuse on a canister grenade, leaned over the landing and loudly counted 'one, two, three' before tossing the grenade towards the barricade. Coughlan cursed fFrench Mullen for unintentionally warning the enemy of the grenade. Both men took cover behind their sandbags as the grenade exploded.[35] Major Vane shouted: 'Who is there? I am Major Vane.'

The only reply was: 'Go to hell.'[36]

During a pause in the firing, Captain Martyn, Corporal Walker and another soldier removed the body of the dead Sherwood Forester who was blocking the breach and crawled through the opening in the wall into the Nurses' Home. They found themselves in the porch area facing a large barricade that almost reached the ceiling. The concussive thud of an exploding grenade showered Captain Martyn and the hallway with debris. The intervening ground between the breached wall and the barricade was swept by rifle fire from the landing. Cover could only be obtained immediately under the barricade. Captain Oates shouted through the breach, 'Are you all right there?'

'Yes, but we will need some bombs,' came the reply.

A satchel of hand grenades was handed through the breached wall. As Captain Oates came through the breach he could see an office doorway. Suddenly the soldier who had entered with Captain Martyn and Corporal Walker bolted and ran out from the doorway near the porch and back towards the hole in the wall. Captain Oates thought the soldier was running away, but as he turned to follow the man, the soldier stumbled and fell near the gap in the wall. Oates bent down and rolled the soldier over; the man had been shot through the heart and must have been dead as he came through the doorway.

The scene Captain Oates stepped into was one of utter chaos. As his eyes grew accustomed to the smoke and dust of the battle he saw he was standing in a lobby. To his right side was the main door of the Nurses' Home that had been barricaded shut. To his left was a wide doorway with an ornamental archway at its top that divided the lobby. Erected in the archway was a barricade that almost reached the apex of the arch. It was constructed of sandbags, stones, bedsteads, mattresses and office furniture. The top of this obstruction was almost in line with the lower landing of the stairway. Opposite to where he stood, he could see a doorway that led into an office. Captain Martyn and Corporal Walker lay on the floor just under the barricade, near the office door. Corporal Walker lobbed a grenade, but the missile failed to clear the top of the barricade and rolled back amongst the British soldiers. The grenade rolled across the floor, its seven-second fuse burning profusely. Martyn rushed forward, seized the bomb and threw it. The grenade cleared the barricade and exploded in the small hallway beyond with a deafening blast.

Captain Oates armed with a Colt automatic pistol opened fire towards the Volunteer position on the landing. Plaster dust choked the men as defenders and attackers opened fire in the small hallway. The smell of cordite was suffocating. In an attempt to outflank the Volunteers' barricade, Captains Martyn and Oates and Corporal Walker crawled on their stomachs into the room beside the lobby. Here Captain Martyn broke the window with his revolver but found it was barred from the outside. They realised they would have to crawl back to the hole in the wall and work their way around the outside of the building. The British officers loaded their weapons before attempting to move back to the breach in the wall.

On the ground floor, Lieutenant Cosgrave opened fire on the British soldiers crouching behind the barricade. Grenades exploded inside the building showering the defenders with bricks and plaster. Cathal Brugha was on the second floor, in the front rooms of the Nurses' Home. The Volunteers hung tenaciously to their position while Brugha urged them on. Walking between the rooms and the landing he continuously risked his life with the casual abandon of those who think they are invincible.

Commandant Ceannt had seen the military occupy the Bakehouse (18) and knew that his line of retreat was in danger of being cut off. Hurrying out the rear door of the Nurses' Home, Ceannt's intention was to call up the sixteen Volunteers positioned over the James's Street entrance (14) as reinforcements. As he left the building, panicky shouts of 'the British are in' filled the air, causing many of the Volunteers to withdraw from their positions. Explosions tore gaps in the roof and amidst the din of battle, the shouts of soldiers and Volunteers echoed throughout the building. These shouts were mistaken for an order to retreat and the Volunteers began to withdraw. In disbelief some retreated down the stairs, firing as they went. As he attempted to cross the hall, a bomb splinter hit Captain fFrench Mullen, wounding him in the leg. Assisted by the other Volunteers, fFrench Mullen and the section withdrew to the back rooms of the Nurses' Home and then on towards the boardroom to join forces with Ceannt. They met in the dormitory between the two buildings and prepared for what they believed would be the final assault on their position.

The barricade at the front door of the Nurses' Home had been left without cover when the Volunteers began to retreat. However, Cathal Brugha had not heard the shouts and he remained on the second floor. Gun at the ready, Brugha moved out onto the landing on the second floor and began to descend the stairway towards the hall.

Chapter 8

Thursday, 27 April 1916
The Final Hours

Lying on the floor behind the barricade on the ground floor of the Nurses' Home, Captain Martyn pulled the pin on a hand grenade and catapulted it over the top towards the Volunteers' now vacated position. The grenade landed on the stairway and began to roll. He could hear it amidst the din of battle as it rolled down the wooden stairs. As the fuse expired, Cathal Brugha, crossing the lower landing, walked into the explosion. His body convulsed as he was thrown against the wall by the force of the blast. He started to collapse on the stairs, his body torn by pieces of shrapnel. Captain Oates then opened fire with his automatic pistol, hitting Brugha as he fell.

Dazed and confused, Brugha began to crawl down the

remaining steps in an attempt to get out of range of the British. The smoke and plaster dust covered his descent. He dragged his shattered body down the remaining steps and across the hallway, leaving a trail of blood smeared on the floor. He hauled himself into a small kitchen off the hallway, propping himself against the wall directly facing the barricade. He raised his 'Peter the Painter' automatic pistol and fired wildly into the barricade and at the ceiling. Bullets ricocheted off the walls. From his position, Brugha prepared to hold off the military single-handed.

Captain Martyn could hear a scraping on the other side of the barricade as Brugha dragged himself along the floor. This was followed by a tremendous blast of gunfire that forced the British officers to lie prone. Pinned down by Brugha's inaccurate but intense fire, Captain Martyn was unable to breach the barricade.

The Volunteers who had withdrawn into the dormitory at the rear of the Nurses' Home prepared for the final assault on their position and a fight to the death. From the top floor of the Nurses' Home, Volunteer J.V. Joyce fired into the ranks of the British soldiers who had taken up position in the Bakehouse. Running short of ammunition he moved from room to room in order to replenish his bandolier. He was amazed to find that he was the last Volunteer on the top storey of the building. As Joyce descended the stairs, he saw Brugha lying on the ground, a mass of wounds, firing at the British soldiers on the other side of the barricade. Joyce moved to Brugha's side and exclaimed, 'Good God, what's happened?' Brugha extracted his pocket watch and requested that it be given to his wife. He then asked for a drink of water. Pocketing the watch, Joyce entered the small kitchen and brought a cup of water back to Brugha. The wounded vice-commandant sipped the water and then told Joyce to get back to the others.[37]

A shout of 'Surrender' came from the far side of the barricade. Brugha said, 'Tell Ceannt I will hold out as long as I can.' Brugha raised his gun and opened fire on the barricade shouting defiantly to the British to come forward and attack. Crouching low, Joyce moved around the foot of the stairs and out into the open courtyard at the rear of the Nurses' Home. Across the yard, a hole had been bored through the wall that led to the offices over James's Street (14). Entering the breach, Joyce found the remainder of the 4th Battalion gathered there.

Lieutenant Cosgrave was arguing with Ceannt that the British had failed to take the Nurses' Home and that they should return and continue the fight. Joyce reported the situation to Ceannt and told him that Brugha was holding the building. The Volunteer commandant was dispirited and his men felt for the first time that defeat and death were possible. The men knelt and said a decade of the Rosary. In the distance they could hear the crack of gunfire. The sound of singing wafted through the air: 'God Save Ireland' could be heard in broken snatches. *God save Ireland, say we proudly, God save Ireland say we all, whether on the scaffold high or the battlefield we die ...* The voice was that of Vice-Commandant Brugha.

Realising that Brugha was managing to hold the position, Ceannt shouted, 'Come on boys.' Rushing back to the barricade in the Nurses' Home, Ceannt and the Volunteers commenced firing at the British troops. The rattle of rifle fire, the smoke and the dust was overwhelming. Ceannt knelt by Brugha's side and spoke in Gaelic. Brugha was then carried out to a small yard at the rear of the building where Lieutenant Cosgrave and Volunteer Joe Doolan attempted to dress his injuries. Both men spent between five and six hours attempting to stem the flow of blood. Brugha was bleeding profusely from a number of wounds and becoming delirious.

As the military threw hand grenades across the barricade, the Volunteers replied with canister bombs. The building was shaken to its foundations after each grenade exploded, threatening to bring the ceiling down on both defender and attacker. However, the Volunteers stood their ground.

Captain Martyn's position was now untenable – he was pinned down and could not advance – so he ordered his remaining troops to withdraw. Captain Martyn and

Corporal Walker scrambled across the floor to the hole in the wall where they turned and gave covering fire so that Captain Oates could make his way to them. They crawled back through the breach and rejoined Major Vane and the remainder of the section. Major Vane and Captain Martyn decided to return to the main force to report. Captain Oates ordered his men to cover the hole in the wall as intense gunfire broke out in the lobby from which they had just come. The sound was deafening in the confined area and the British expected an assault on their position. To the dismay of Captain Oates, the untrained recruits of the Sherwood Foresters bolted, leaving him on his own.[38]

The officer decided to take the remaining hand grenades and hold his position until his fellow officers returned. Every two to three minutes, he lobbed a grenade through the breach into the lobby beyond. The noise was deafening and after each explosion the Irish Volunteers opened fire in order to repulse any attempt by the British to storm their position. Captain Oates was almost out of bombs when Martyn returned and ordered him to fall back. Word had been sent down the line that the transport column was no longer under fire and that an attempt to cross the bridge was underway. Before the two officers left their position they decided to throw the remaining grenades through the breach. Retreating through the wards full of terrified elderly patients, the two officers met an embarrassed Corporal Walker and another soldier who, having realised that Captain Oates was alone, were returning to lend him assistance.

In the meantime, a Volunteer named James Foran, who had been occupying the frontage of the South Dublin Union (14) and had not come under direct fire from the British forces assaulting the Nurses' Home, decided to move through the buildings at the front of the Union in an attempt to link up with Commandant Ceannt and the other Volunteers. Hearing noises outside the building that he thought might be other Volunteers, he opened the front door of the administrative offices. He was spotted by a section of British soldiers near the Bakehouse (18). Foran raised his .45 Webley revolver and opened fire. He then ducked back inside and bolted the door. He ran through the holes that had been bored through the internal walls and exited near the Bakehouse at the rear of the Nurses' Home. In the Nurses' Home he found Ceannt and the remaining Volunteers and asked if they should surrender or if it was a fight to the finish. Ceannt replied that it was a fight to the finish.[39]

Foran and Robert Evans climbed the stairs to take up a firing position that overlooked the courtyard. Suddenly Foran was pulled from behind. 'My God, I am shot', exclaimed Evans as he collapsed. Foran lifted his wounded comrade into a ward and placed him on a bed. Foran then opened a window and fired into the ranks of the attacking British soldiers. Nearby, Irish Volunteers Peadar Doyle and Seán McGlynn became detached from their allies and took refuge on a rooftop. Both men lay on their backs in the roof valley under continuous machine-gun fire from the Royal Hospital. At 7 p.m. a party of British soldiers moved from the convent (8) towards the Nurses' Home (10). In the dwindling light of the day they fired on some of their own men who were at that moment attempting to storm the front of the Nurses' Home. Anticipating the confusion outside in the front courtyard, Commandant Ceannt ordered his men to fire into the ranks of the attackers.

'Retire men,' called out a British officer, 'we are sur-rounded.' Both groups of British soldiers retreated to safer positions.

From 7.30 p.m. to 9.30 p.m. the battle for the Union raged across the barrier. Volunteers lay flat on the landing of the stairs firing with revolvers, automatics and rifles out over the barricade. The continuous barrage prevented the British from storming the building. Meanwhile, 'A' company of the Sherwood Foresters had succeeded in clearing the left and front flanks of the column near Rialto Bridge. Captain Martyn's attack on the Nurses' Home had distracted the Volunteers so that firing on the column had practically ceased and it was decided that it was safe to bring the wagons over the bridge at a gallop. The horses charged the bridge, the wheels of the wagons scraping the cobbled stones. The drivers of the wagons brandished loaded rifles in one hand, while holding the reins in the other. The transport crossed safely with only one bullet hole appearing in a single vehicle.[40] The main body of troops followed this and soon the entire column reached the main gates of the Royal Hospital. A message was relayed back to the sections providing covering fire within the Union to withdraw to Rialto Bridge. The left flank withdrew without incident but the Irish Volunteers constantly harried the right flank. Lieutenant Monk Gibbon later wrote of the withdrawal:

> The convoy is formed up and we move off. It is doubtful if we need ever have been halted. It is 7 p.m. now. I am filthy, deaf from firing in the little room and most of my ammunition has gone. Someone gives me a lemon to suck. We continue along the South Circular Road.[41]

Both sections of British troops regrouped near the bridge by 9.45 p.m. and immediately marched towards the Royal Hospital arriving at 10.15 p.m. They billeted for the night on the floors of the Hospital's Great Hall and around the altar in the baroque chapel. Though many slept, others reflected on the past days' actions, the losses to the battalion and the fighting that they would face in the coming days.

The skyline had turned a blood red as flames relentlessly consumed the metropolis. Dublin city was burning.

Chapter 9

Intermission

Crown forces made no further assaults on the South Dublin Union and by midday on Friday the Volunteers realised that the British had completely withdrawn from the complex. The days that followed were uneventful except for the sporadic sniper fire that came from the roof of the Royal Hospital, Kilmainham.

The British contingent that had attempted to occupy the Bakehouse (18) retired, having received orders from Captain Martyn on Thursday evening. Removing their boots to prevent noise, they rushed back across the courtyard to a place of refuge on the east side of the square. During this withdrawal, a British soldier became detached from his unit and realising that he was pinned down and unable to escape, took cover in the nearby carpentry shop.

He stayed in the building overnight and most of Friday as Volunteer snipers sporadically opened fire. Later, as a hearse arrived and Union patients placed the dead body of a British soldier in a coffin, the soldier hiding in the carpentry shop saw his means of escape. Stealthily moving from cover, he climbed into an empty coffin beside that of the corpse. The two coffins were then loaded onto a cart in full view of the Volunteers who permitted the vehicle to leave the area as it travelled under a Red Cross flag. Later, the khaki-clad Lazarus emerged from his tomb to the astonishment of civilian onlookers.[42]

Vice-Commandant Cathal Brugha was in a serious condition and Ceannt requested assistance from Father Gerhard. Wearing his priest's stole, Father Gerhard led a procession carrying Brugha on a stretcher from the Nurses' Home to one of the Union medical wards.

At the same time the Union officials applied to the military for permission to remove Volunteer Dan Mc-Carthy to Merrion Square for an X-ray. He had suffered a serious stomach wound and had been accommodated in a ward at the Union since Monday. In response, the military stated that if he could be moved to Merrion Square, he was fit enough to be moved to the military hospital in Dublin Castle. As McCarthy was loaded into the ambulance, he saw another Volunteer was with him and immediately recognised Cathal Brugha. Both men were transferred to hospital in Dublin Castle. Brugha was put in the care of Sir William Taylor and McCarthy was put in the care of Surgeon Haughton. Having consulted an X-ray of McCarthy's wound, the surgeon decided not to operate and said, 'Let sleeping dogs lie.'[43] The surgeon believed that rest and good care would be enough to pull McCarthy through. When the military gave orders for the removal of McCarthy to Kilmainham Gaol, the surgeon's protests were ignored and the Volunteer was incarcerated in the Gaol.[44]

Having examined Brugha, the physicians deemed that he would not survive and he was released into the care of his family. He had suffered twenty-five wounds. Of these, five were considered very dangerous having perforated a number of arteries, nine were considered very serious and eleven were superficial. However, Brugha survived, cheating both death and the British authorities.

Back in the Union the remaining Volunteers refortified their positions. Although his garrison was badly depleted, Ceannt remained calm and encouraged his men. Since Wednesday they had noticed the red glow of fires appearing over the city. They had also heard the sound of artillery mingling with the relentless sound of both rifle and machine-gun fire. No dispatches had been received from Volunteer headquarters at the General Post Office in Sackville Street since Tuesday morning.

In the Union outpost at the Marrowbone Lane Distillery, the Irish Volunteer garrison were subjected to incessant sniper fire from British crown forces hiding behind a barricade they had erected near Echlin Street on Tuesday. Communication with Commandant Ceannt had been cut off so he was unaware that the Marrowbone Lane garrison had thwarted a number of British assaults at the canal end of the Union complex. On Saturday night Volunteer Robert Holland ventured out of the distillery under the cover of darkness to collect the arms and ammunition of the fallen British soldiers. Acting with a number of others, Holland managed to acquire a considerable amount of ammunition and more than ten Lee Enfield rifles. When Holland returned to the distillery, Volunteer Jack Saul mentioned to him that he had heard digging outside the gate. Both Volunteers stood ready as they heard the noise of chains rattling. They shouted a challenge but the noise continued. Both men opened fire through the gate into the darkness. A few moments later Volunteer Sergeant Kerrigan appeared and informed them that they had shot and killed a horse belonging to a local trader, 'Mocky' Keogh.[45]

The garrison within the distillery had been reinforced by men and women who, realising the Rising was taking place, joined them throughout the week. On Saturday the total number of troops inside stood at a hundred men and forty women of Cumann na mBan. They had ample supplies of food and ammunition and morale was high. On Saturday morning British troops had withdrawn out of range of the distillery, but the Volunteers were told to 'stand to' as a massed attack was expected. However, the day was uneventful and the men stood down from their positions. News filtered in to the distillery that British troops had suffered heavy casualties in the city and that Volunteers still remained entrenched in their positions. Members of Cumann na mBan baked cakes and a ceilidhe was organised for Sunday evening.

Members of the 4th Battalion of the Irish Volunteers under the command of Commandant Éamonn Ceannt, had successfully repulsed numerous attacks by superior numbers of British crown forces and held their position within the South Dublin Union and its outlying posts for six consecutive days. Sunday, would be their seventh.

Chapter 10

Surrender

At 2 a.m. on Friday 28 April 1916, General Sir John Grenfell Maxwell arrived at the North Wall in Dublin city. The night sky was illuminated as the buildings on Sackville Street (O'Connell Street) burned fiercely and the sound of gunfire echoed throughout the deserted streets. Accompanied by a number of staff officers, General Maxwell made his way to the Royal Hospital where he conferred with Major General Friend and Brigadier General Lowe. At this meeting Lowe was instructed to tighten the cordon around the Volunteer positions on Sackville Street.

Patrick Pearse, commander-in-chief of the Irish Volunteers, had initiated contact with Brigadier General W.H.M. Lowe, commander of the British forces in Dublin, and at 1.40 p.m. on Saturday 29 April. Lowe conveyed a note of reply:

A woman has come in and tells me you wish to negotiate with me. I am prepared to receive you in Britain Street at the north end of Moore Street provided that you surrender unconditionally. You will proceed up Moore Street accompanied only by the woman who brings you this note under a white flag.[46]

At 3.30 p.m., Patrick Pearse accompanied by Nurse Elizabeth O'Farrell met with Brigadier General Lowe. Handwritten notes ordering full surrender were penned by Pearse, and Nurse O'Farrell delivered them to some of the garrison commanders around Dublin city. It was the beginning of the end.

At 10 a.m. on Sunday, Commandant Thomas Mc-Donagh of the Irish Volunteers, along with Father Aloysius and Father Albert from Church Street, were admitted to the South Dublin Union. They informed Ceannt that Pearse had surrendered in order to save the citizens of Dublin from further suffering. Having conversed with the envoys, Commandant Ceannt addressed his men and relayed to them the decisions of headquarters. Suggestions were made that the Volunteers should attempt to evade capture, as there was no military guard. However, the majority made a case for complete surrender because they had stood together throughout the week and should continue to do so to the end. The envoys left and proceeded to the garrison at the Marrowbone Lane Distillery where the news of surrender was greeted with dismay.

Later on Sunday afternoon a British officer (possibly Sir Francis Fletcher Vane) accompanied by a member of the clergy arrived to converse with Ceannt. The officer said: 'You had a fine position here.'

Ceannt replied: 'Yes, and we made full use of it. Not alone did we hold your army for six days but shook it to its foundation.'[47]

Ceannt ordered his men to fall in and assemble at the square in the Union. When they had done so Ceannt was told to form up all his men. The British officer looked surprised when Ceannt replied that this was all of his men, 'forty-one all told'. Lieutenant Cosgrave mobilised the men and his words of command could be clearly heard. They marched to the Marrowbone Lane Distillery and waited there until the garrison emerged to join their ranks. The 4th Battalion then marched under the command of Commandant Éamonn Ceannt to St Patrick's Park, adjacent to St Patrick's Cathedral. Father Augustine waited for Ceannt's men to arrive at the park. He wrote:

> They did not arrive and I began to wonder what was causing the delay. In about fifteen minutes, however, we saw the South Dublin Union garrison marching in, and at once my eye caught sight of the splendid figure

of the leader. The whole column marched splendidly, with guns slung from their left shoulders and their hands swinging freely at their sides. They wore no look of defeat, but rather of victory. It seems as if they had come out to celebrate a triumph and were marching to receive a decoration. Ceannt was in the middle of the front section with one man on either side. But my eyes were riveted on him so tall was his form, so noble his bearing, and so manly his stride. He was indeed the worthy captain of a brave band who had fought a clean fight for Ireland.[48]

At the cathedral, the Volunteers grounded their arms under their commandant's command. Weapons were unloaded and collected by the military and placed in lorries. Joining up with the Volunteer battalion that had occupied Jacob's biscuit factory, the Volunteers were then marched under military escort to Richmond barracks, passing the Union on the way. In the poorer areas they were greeted with cheers and wishes of luck, but as they neared the barracks the tone changed and the crowds were more threatening and abusive.

On arrival at Richmond barracks, about sixty men were locked in each room with no furniture and little ventilation. The only sanitary provision was a large bucket in the corner of the room. For breakfast buckets containing tea and a basket of hard biscuits were distributed. The biscuits were tumbled out onto the floor and empty bully-beef tins were used as tea containers. Later in the day, police from 'G' division of the Dublin Metropolitan Police arrived and began to identify those who had played a prominent role in the week's insurrection. Commandant Ceannt and Lieutenant Cosgrave were singled out, separated and marched away for interrogation.

Those Volunteers, such as James Burke, who had been taken prisoner early in the week, had been taken to Kilmainham police station. They were questioned by military intelligence officers and then moved to Richmond barracks and placed in the guardroom. From there they were conveyed to Kilmainham Gaol. Burke recalled:

> We were brought over to Kilmainham Gaol, where some drunken soldiery of the Dublin Fusiliers immediately set upon us, kicking us, beating us and threatening us with bayonets. We looked at one another the next morning and thought we were dead. The Dublin Fusiliers were the worst of the lot.
>
> The soldiers threatened the Volunteers throughout the night and shouted, 'Who is Sinn Féin?' They seemed to think that 'Sinn Féin' was the name of the Volunteers' leader. The English soldiers were mostly decent. Most of them were young fellows who did not know one end of a rifle from the other as far as I could see.[49]

The Volunteers were taken from Richmond barracks, marched to the quays and then sent to Knutsford. They were then transferred to Frongoch prison camp in Wales. Volunteer Paddy Morrissey who had been wounded in the leg on Monday had been transferred to hospital under military escort. He escaped from hospital soon afterwards in a milk cart. He was never formally arrested.

Some time after the battle, Major Sir Francis Fletcher Vane walked through the shattered remains of the Nurses' Home and wrote, 'I am sorry for our poor fellows who were killed. They fought splendidly. So did the enemy.'[50]

Chapter 11

May 1916
Trial and Retribution

On 3 May 1916, Commandant Éamonn Ceannt was tried by field general court-martial in the gymnasium of Richmond barracks, Inchicore. His trial lasted two days. The presiding judges were Brigadier General C.G. Blackader (President), Lieutenant Colonel G. German and Lieutenant Colonel W.J. Kent. The trial was held in secret, behind closed doors. The charges against him stated that he:

Did an act to wit; did take part in an armed rebellion and in the waging of war against his Majesty the King, such act being of such a nature as to be calculated to be prejudicial to the Defence to the Realm and being done with the intention and for the purpose of assisting the enemy.[51]

Ceannt pleaded not guilty to the charges put before him.

William G. Wylie was appointed as counsel for the prosecution. Born in Dublin, Wylie had been called to the Irish bar in 1905 and in 1914 he was appointed King's Counsel. During the rebellion he was stationed in Trinity College as a member of the Officer Training Corps and had accepted the surrender of many of those he was now going to prosecute. In Ceannt's case, Wylie called the only witness for the prosecution, a Major J.E. Armstrong of the First Royal Enniskillen Fusiliers. Major Armstrong had been present at the surrender of Ceannt in St Patrick's Park on 30 April, but this was the first time he had actually seen the defendant. Armstrong implied that Ceannt had surrendered as one of the party from the Jacob's biscuit factory and had therefore been involved in firing at British troops in the area. He also stated that Ceannt held the rank of commandant and was armed at the time of the surrender.[52]

The evidence provided by Major Armstrong was circumstantial and Ceannt denied being a member of the garrison at Jacob's. The court was adjourned until the following day as Ceannt requested a number of witnesses. One of these, Thomas McDonagh, had already been executed on 3 May. Ceannt called John MacBride as a witness in his defence. MacBride testified that Ceannt was not part of the Jacob's garrison and two others, Richard Davis and Patrick Sweeny, also testified that Ceannt was not at Jacob's.

Ceannt claimed that he had surrendered in the area of St Patrick's Park and had arrived there at the head of two bodies of Volunteers, but that he was only in command of one. He declared that the sworn testimonies of his witnesses proved that he was not in the vicinity of Jacob's and so had not fired on British troops. In his final address to the court he said: 'I claim at least that there is reasonable doubt and the benefit of the doubt should be given to the accused.'[53] The court did not accept his plea and returned the verdict of guilty – the punishment was death by firing squad. Before leaving his men in Richmond barracks, Ceannt gave instructions that each man was to make the best defence possible.

On the evening of 5 May, Ceannt was transferred from Richmond barracks to Kilmainham Gaol to await his execution. On 6 May, General Sir John Maxwell, Commander of the British forces in Ireland, confirmed the court verdict of guilty. The day before his execution, Ceannt wrote a statement from his cell in Kilmainham about the action in the South Dublin Union:

I leave for the guidance of other Irish revolutionaries who may tread the path which I have trod this advice: never to treat with the enemy, never to surrender to his mercy, but fight to a finish. I see nothing gained but grave disaster caused, by the surrender which has marked the end of the Irish insurrection of 1916 – so far at least as Dublin is concerned. The enemy has not cherished one generous thought for those who, with little hope, with poor equipment, and weak in numbers, withstood his forces for one glorious week. Ireland has shown she is a nation. This generation can claim to have raised sons as brave as any that went before. And in the years to come Ireland will honour those who risked all for her honour at Easter in 1916. I bear no ill will towards those against whom I fought. I have found the common soldiers and the higher officers humane and companionable, even the English who were actually in the fight against us. Thank God soldiering for Ireland has opened my heart and made me see poor humanity where I expected to see only scorn and reproach. I have met the man who escaped from me by a ruse under the Red Cross. But I do not regret having withheld my fire. He gave me cakes!

I wish to record the magnificent gallantry and fearless calm determination of the men who fought with me. All, all, were simply splendid. Even I knew no fear nor panic and shrunk from no risk even as I shrink not now for a moment in the morning. His will be done. All are very kind. My poor wife saw me yesterday and bore up so my warden told me – even after she left my presence. Poor Áine and Ronan. God is their only shield now that I am removed. And God is a better shield than I. I have just seen Áine, Nell, Richard and Mick and bade them a conditioned goodbye. Even now they hope!

Éamonn Ceannt[54]

At dawn on Monday 8 May, 1916, Éamonn Ceannt was led out to the stonebreaker's yard in Kilmainham Gaol. His hands had been tied behind his back, he had been blindfolded and a piece of white paper had been placed over his heart to act as a target. He held a crucifix in his tied hands given to him by Father Augustine. As Ceannt was placed sitting on an upturned wooden soapbox, a British army officer moved forward and asked him to stretch his legs out. The firing squad entered the yard after the prisoner and took up their firing position, six kneeling and six standing. On command the firing squad made ready, presented arms and fired. Ceannt tumbled over as the bullets found their mark. However, he was still alive. The officer moved forward, withdrew his revolver and performed the final *coup de grâce* with a single shot to

Ceannt's head. As Father Augustine administered extreme unction, he retrieved the cross from Ceannt's hands and saw that it was spattered with blood.[55] The squad were marched out of the yard, grounded their weapons and the spent cartridges were collected. They then cleaned their rifles. All the firing squads were drawn from the Sherwood Forester Regiment. They had suffered the heaviest casualties in their engagements at Mount Street Bridge and also at the South Dublin Union. The regimental history of the Sherwood Forester Regiment states that all those who were executed met their fate bravely.[56]

Official records show that Éamonn Ceannt was executed by firing squad between 3:45 a.m. and 4:05 a.m. Captain H.M. Whitehead of the 7th Battalion Sherwood Foresters, acting as Assistant Provost Marshal, signed the confirmation of Ceannt's death.[57] Brigadier J. Young issued a memorandum from Irish command headquarters at Parkgate Street in relation to the procedure for the burial of those who were executed:

After each prisoner has been shot, a medical officer will certify that he is dead, and his body will be immediately removed to an ambulance, with a label pinned on his breast giving his name. When the ambulance is full, it will be sent to Arbour Hill detention barracks, entering by the gate at the Garrison Chapel. The party will put the bodies close alongside one another in the grave, cover them quickly in quicklime and commence filling the grave. One of the officers with his party is to keep a note of the position of each body in the grave, taking the name from the label. A priest will attend for the funeral service.[58]

Between 3–12 May 1916, fourteen men were executed at Kilmainham Gaol and removed to Arbour Hill detention barracks for burial. General Sir John Grenfell Maxwell, officer in command, was adamant that the bodies of those executed should not be released to their families. In an attempt to prevent the graves being turned into a martyr's shrine, the executed men were buried in quicklime and without coffins.

On 11 May 1916, General Maxwell wrote a memorandum to Herbert Asquith in relation to Ceannt:

This man was one of the signatories to the declaration of Irish Independence. He was on the executive committee and central council of the Irish Volunteers and attended all their meetings. He was an extremist in his views and identified himself with all pro-German movements. He held the rank of commandant in the rebel army and was in command at the South Dublin Union in the capture of which the British troops suffered heavily, losing both officers and men. He was armed at the time of his surrender.[59]

Éamonn Ceannt had carried out his orders to the last detail. He held his position within the South Dublin Union, inflicting heavy casualties on his attackers. He fought the British government on the battlefield and in the courtroom of Richmond barracks – in both cases, the odds were stacked heavily against him. And, in the end, he reluctantly obeyed the order to surrender, knowing that as a signatory of the Proclamation of the Republic, he had voluntarily signed his own death warrant.

Chapter 12

Murder and Mayhem at the Guinness Brewery?

On Monday 12 June, 1916, a general court-martial assembled at Richmond barracks in Dublin to try Company Quartermaster Sergeant Robert Flood of the 5th Battalion Royal Dublin Fusiliers.

Quartermaster Sergeant Robert Flood, a career soldier, enlisted in the Royal Dublin Fusiliers on 11 January 1899, aged fourteen years and nine months. He saw service at home, in Egypt, India and in the Mediterranean Expeditionary Force. The accused was standing trial for the murders of Lieutenant Algernon Lucas of the 2nd King Edward's Horse and William John Rice, an employee of the Guinness Brewery on James's Street. The series of tragic events that led to the deaths of these two men took place during the panic and confusion that gripped the area as the battle raged within the South Dublin Union.[60]

The Guinness Brewery on James's Street stood in close proximity to the South Dublin Union. The brewing complex covered over sixty-five acres and consisted of offices, brewing facilities and storage areas. From their vantage point in the Guinness storehouse, a few employees could see the buildings burning on Sackville Street and Capel Street. In order to protect the Bond Street boundary of the Brewery from possible attack by the Irish Volunteers positioned at the Jameson's Distillery on Marrowbone Lane, the management of the brewery arranged with the British military for a small picket of soldiers to be deployed in the Robert Street Malt Store near the Grand Canal harbour. Colonel Williams promised to reinforce this small section as soon as more men became available.

Nine men and one officer of the Royal Dublin Fusiliers took up position throughout the Malt Store on the evening of Friday 28 April at 9 p.m. Their officer, Captain Charles McNamara, 5th RDF, was ordered to occupy the building, not to answer sniper fire unless there were attempts to enter the brewery, not to open any windows and to hold the place overnight. The soldiers were placed at strategic points throughout the building and were ordered to watch a small footbridge at the harbour, as this is where they believed an attack would emanate from. The sound of rifle and machine-gun fire was continuous and the boom of artillery added to the fears of the staff and military who expected to be attacked at any moment. McNamara was told that the only brewery officials on duty that night were three night watchmen who would have lamps.

The sound of gunfire steadily increased outside the Malt Store, so it was arranged to leave the brewery in darkness in order to escape the possibility of sniping. It was a very dark night and the Malt Store was an eerie place, illuminated only by the fires in Dublin city. Sinister shadows were cast across the halls and stairwells as the soldiers patrolled the building, their boots echoing on the stone floors accompanied by the rattle of their military accoutrements. During the night it was decided to relieve Captain McNamara and at 11 p.m., Captain A.R. Rotheram of the 10th Cavalry Reserve arrived and presented 2nd Lieutenant Algernon Lucas of the 2nd King Edward's Horse. As Lieutenant Lucas prepared to take command, Captain McNamara related the orders to the lieutenant in the presence of Quartermaster Sergeant Robert Flood. Captain Rotheram and Captain McNamara withdrew from the Malt Store leaving the picket alone in the darkness.[61]

Later that night Captain Rotheram was contacted by telephone at Kingsbridge Station by Lieutenant Henry Worswick to say that Mr Rice, a night watchman, had failed to return from a patrol to the Malt Store. Captain Rotheram ordered that no action be taken until daylight the following day. However, Lieutenant Worswick, who was also an officer in the 2nd King Edward's Horse, and a night watchman named Dockeray made their way towards the Malt House to investigate. They also failed to return.

The following day it was revealed that the two officers and the two employees of the brewery were shot dead in the Malt Store on the orders of Quartermaster Sergeant Robert Flood. At the subsequent trial the events of the night were revealed. The quartermaster sergeant grew suspicious of Lieutenant Lucas after he caught him attempting to open a window on the third floor. He reiterated the orders they had received but Lieutenant Lucas told the sergeant that he was in charge. Suspecting that the officer was a 'Sinn Féiner' and was attempting to signal to the enemy, the sergeant shone his torch at the officer and ordered his colleagues to cover the officer with their rifles. At this point, Mr Rice appeared and he too found himself covered by five rifles. Both men were searched. Sergeant Flood believed that the two men were 'Sinn Féiners' who were attempting to signal to the enemy in the South Dublin Union. He told them they were going to be shot. Lieutenant Lucas asked to say his prayers and knelt on the ground. As he rose the officer pleaded, 'Don't fire sergeant; I am only a poor farmer's son.' He was crying and when asked why, he replied he was thinking of his wife and child. Sergeant Flood ordered the officer to remove his coat so as not to disgrace its insignia. The officer was placed against a wall and the order to fire was given by the sergeant. A volley of shots rang out in the stairwell and the officer collapsed on the floor. A second order was given to fire at Mr Rice and he too fell to the floor. He was still alive, so Private Maurice McCarthy reloaded and fired again into the body.

After half an hour the picket made their way down to the second floor where they heard footsteps approaching their position. The order to 'Halt' was shouted out twice by Sergeant Flood but it was ignored. The sergeant turned on his electric torch and saw an officer (Lt Worswick) and civilian (Mr Dockeray) standing before them. Sergeant Flood covered the men with his rifle and called to his colleagues for assistance. They soon arrived and searched the two men. They were asked what they were doing in the building and both men refused to answer. Suddenly Lieutenant Worswick lunged at Quartermaster Sergeant Flood, knocking him to the ground. The other soldiers opened fire killing Lieutenant Worswick and Mr Dockeray.

The following morning the soldiers reported the killings to their superior officers.

At the trial, the prosecution was conducted by Major E.G. Kimber, DSO, who relayed the facts of the case to the court. The defence council, Mr Henry Hanna, KC, questioned Quartermaster Sergeant Robert Flood:

'At the time you ordered the first two to be shot, did you honestly believe it was necessary for the safety of yourself and your men?'

'I did.'

'Did you think it was necessary for the purpose of carrying out your military duty?'

'I did.'[62]

Shortly afterwards the president of the court-martial announced that the accused, Quartermaster Sergeant Robert Flood, had been found not guilty. The court erupted into applause.

Many excused the incident as an unfortunate event brought about by inexperienced soldiers who were suffering from nervous exhaustion. On 16 June 1916 the following statement was published:

Messers Arthur Guinness, Sons and Co., Limited, are authorised by Lord Cheylesmore to state that there was nothing to justify any suggestion that either Mr Dockeray or Mr Rice was in any way connected with, or in sympathy with, the Sinn Féin rebellion. He regrets that any such idea should have arisen.

(Signed) H.W. Renny Tailyour

Managing Director[63]

As news of this and other civilian deaths caused by the military authorities filtered out by word of mouth and through *The Irish Times*, public opinion changed from apathy to outrage. The military were reluctant to investigate these deaths and although subsequent coroner's reports and trials were carried out to appease the public, they often ended without prosecution. A possible reason behind this failure to investigate is contained in a dispatch to the secretary of war on 26 May 1916 written by General Sir John Maxwell:

Allegations on the behaviour of the troops brought to my notice are being most carefully inquired into. I am glad to say they are few in number, and these are not borne out by direct evidence. I wish to emphasise that the responsibility for the loss of life, however it occurred, the destruction of property, and other losses, rests entirely with those who engineered this revolt, and who, at a time when the Empire is engaged in a gigantic struggle, invited the assistance and co-operation of the Germans.[64]

Almost a month after his trial Sergeant Flood was transferred to the Royal Berkshire Regiment and later attained the rank of CSM. He was killed in action at Salonika on 9 May 1917, aged thirty-three. There is no mention of his court-martial or his acquittal in his service records.

Chapter 13

Aftermath

The following general order was issued to the troops by General Sir John Grenfell Maxwell, general commander of the British forces in Ireland on 1 May 1916:

> I desire to thank the troops who have been engaged in the city of Dublin for their splendid behaviour under the trying conditions of street fighting which I found it necessary to order them to undertake. Owing to the excellent direction of the officers and the tireless effort of the troops, all the surviving rebels in Dublin have now surrendered unconditionally. I especially wish to express my gratitude to those Irish regiments that have so largely helped to crush this Rising.[65]

No special list of honours was issued in relation to the services rendered by the military during the 1916 Rising. On 20 June 1916 in the Houses of Parliament, London, Sir J.D. Rees asked Under Secretary of State for War Harold Tennant what recognition was to be given to the officers and men of the Sherwood Foresters who lost their lives and received wounds in the recent street fighting in Dublin, where they acquitted themselves with the coolness of seasoned troops, as well as with gallantry, under circumstances calculated to try experienced veterans? He asked if recognition was to be given precisely on the same footing as for ordinary service? Mr Tennant replied that recognition had already been given and that he did not know if any further acknowledgment would be granted. He reiterated that the Prime Minister had expressed gratitude.

The *London Gazette* carried the names of soldiers who were mentioned in dispatches and Captain Michael (Micky) Cleeve Martyn of the Nottingham and Derbyshire Regiment received the Military Cross for his actions. Of the fifty-two honours and awards given out for the Rising, fifteen were awarded to the men of the Sherwood Forester Regiment, and of the eighteen highest awards issued, ten were awarded to the Sherwood Forester Regiment.

The exact number of crown casualties for the battle for the South Dublin Union is difficult to determine as a number of men from various regiments were engaged in the fighting during the week.

The Royal Irish Regiment lists two officers and five men killed in action and one officer and six men wounded. The regimental history of the Sherwood Foresters gives the relatively low number of three men killed in action and seven wounded during the fighting at the Union. Many of those wounded returned to England and were subsequently discharged from the army only to succumb to their wounds later. Of the total military casualties of the entire Rising, the Sherwood Foresters suffered the most – 214 officers and men killed or wounded, many of these in the engagement at Mount Street Bridge. A complete and accurate list may never be compiled as many of those killed in action are listed as being killed at home with no definite time or place of death recorded. The Rising in Dublin and its casualties was considered a comparatively minor affair to the British Army High Command. However, their attitude to warfare was to dramatically change with the onslaught of the Somme offensive of July 1916. The battle for Dublin became a distant memory to many as the Somme united British and Irish families, not through victory or defeat, but through their losses.

In the weeks and months that followed the in-surrection in Dublin, the British troops who remained in Ireland were dispatched throughout the country as martial law was strictly enforced. Later, many of these regiments found themselves in action on the Western Front in Europe. Captain Micky Martyn fought with the Sherwood Foresters, receiving the Distinguished Service Order (DSO). He was later attached to the 6th Battalion of the Royal Leicestershire Regiment and was reported missing in action in August 1918. It was later discovered that he had been taken prisoner by the Germans and he was repatriated that same year. Martyn died on 13 June 1978.

Captain John Sherbrook Coape Oates was wounded twice in action on his return to France and Belgium. He was awarded the DSO and his father, Lieutenant Colonel Oates received his DSO at the same investiture at Buckingham Palace. Captain Oates continued his military service, serving with the Royal Artillery in the Second World War. He died at home on 24 February 1978.

The young lieutenant, Monk Gibbon, survived the war and became a well-known writer, recording his experiences in Dublin 1916 in a book entitled *Inglorious Soldier*.

The executions of the leaders of the Rising had caused revulsion amongst the populace and public opinion began to swing in favour of the Irish Volunteers who had been incarcerated abroad. By December 1916, Volunteer Peadar Doyle, like many others, found himself imprisoned in Lewes jail in England. The Irish Volunteers formed a committee to fight for their recognition as prisoners of war. They lobbied the authorities and as time progressed conditions for the prisoners slowly improved.

Education and work details were organised by the prisoners. The governor of the prison was impressed with painting work that had been carried out within the jail by the prisoners. He enquired if it would be possible for the prisoners to paint his house and after thinking the matter over, the prisoners submitted an estimate and the work commenced. The governor was very pleased with the standard of workmanship and when the job was finished he brought his friends to see it. It was some time afterwards that he realised that the doors and panels had been painted green, white and orange. In another small act of rebellion a member of the work crew was selected to distract the guard while the painters wrote 'This house has been decorated by the Irish Prisoners of War 1917', before it was covered in wallpaper.[66]

Many prisoners were released by late 1917 or early 1918 and on their return to Ireland, they found that attitudes to the Rising had shifted and that public opinion had changed dramatically from condemnation to admiration.

Major Sir Francis Fletcher Vane, the British officer who had led the attack on the South Dublin Union on the

Thursday afternoon, found himself deprived of his rank and dismissed from the army by the end of May 1916. He wrote:

> This combat remains in my memory for it made me acquainted with Mr William Cosgrave (now president of the Free State) who was commanding against me. This occurred during a short truce, when both sides joined to save two old men who happened to get into the line of fire. It is pleasant to remember that Cosgrave and I retain our friendship to this day and he has helped me in my efforts to lessen the troubles wrought by war. For this engagement I was commended by the Brigadier General Maconchy. Report was held back on account of my exposé of the Skeffington murders and Sir John Maxwell held back General Maconchy's report.[67]

During the Rising, a number of atrocities took place that the military authorities tried to cover up. At Portobello barracks in Dublin, Captain Bowen Colthurst executed three innocent civilians without trial. The three men, Francis Sheehy Skeffington, Patrick McIntyre and Thomas Dickson were executed on Wednesday 26 April. After the events of Easter week, Major Vane attempted to contact British High Command in Dublin to report the actions of

Captain Bowen Colthurst, but he failed to reach General Maxwell. He spoke to an intelligence officer who seemed uninterested. Royal Engineers were sent from Dublin Castle to Portobello barracks in order to repair the wall where the three men had been shot. This was a deliberate attempt to cover up the murders and an admission by crown forces that they were aware of the incident. Finally, as a result of a communication to the military authorities in London made by Major Vane, Captain Bowen Colthurst was placed under 'open' arrest on 6 May and subsequently on 11 May under 'close' arrest. On 6 and 7 June 1916, Captain Bowen Colthurst was tried by court-martial in Dublin for the murder of Francis Sheehy Skeffington and was found guilty but insane. He served one year in prison, was released and spent the remainder of his life in Canada as a successful banker.

Though Sir Francis Fletcher Vane received the admiration of the Irish people for his honesty and integrity in relation to the events at Portobello barracks, he spent the remainder of his life campaigning for a review of his dismissal and reinstatement. His appeals to the military authorities were without success. He spent the remainder of his life living abroad.

British soldiers shot many unarmed civilians during the Rising, and later, Sir John Grenfell Maxwell admitted in a newspaper article that atrocities had taken place in

Dublin during Easter Week. The files on many of these atrocities were assigned to the dusty annals of an archive until 2001, when the British government finally released the official papers into the public domain.

Though the everyday work of the South Dublin Union continued during Easter week, the minute books of the workhouse were not updated until May 1916. Within these pages there is mention of the damage to the buildings and the complex that occurred during its occupation. After the Volunteers vacated the grounds of the South Dublin Union, the gates were opened and the local populace went through the buildings seeking mementos of the week's events. Many items were taken that had no connection with the Rising, including many personal items belonging to nurses who were resident in the Nurses' Home. The nurses were later compensated for their losses. The minute books fail to mention the names of any patients who were killed or died of natural causes during that week. The poor and destitute of Dublin who entered the Union became nameless and were forgotten. The only reference to their existence and tragic deaths are in the personal recollections of those who fought on both sides during the Rising.

Lieutenant W.T. Cosgrave was sentenced to death for his involvement in the South Dublin Union; later that sentence was commuted to imprisonment. He was sent to a series of prisons in England and was released in 1917. He returned to a changed Ireland and entered the political fray that preceded the Irish War of Independence. Having accepted the Anglo-Irish Treaty in 1922, his decision brought him into direct conflict with old friends and colleagues. After the deaths of Arthur Griffith and Michael Collins in 1922, William T. Cosgrave became chairman of the Provisional Government in July and president of the Dáil in August of that year. As the Civil War raged throughout the country, Cosgrave was considered by many to be ruthless in his defence of the state against his former republican colleagues. In 1923 a new political party called Cumann na nGaedheal was established with Cosgrave as its leader. He remained in power for a decade and later became leader of Fine Gael until he retired from politics in 1944. Cosgrave died peacefully in November 1965 aged eighty-five and is buried in Goldenbridge cemetery, Dublin.

Having survived his wounds, Cathal Brugha was appointed chief-of-staff of the Irish Republican Army in 1917. On 21 January 1919, at the first sitting of the Dáil, Brugha was elected as acting president because Éamonn de Valera and other Sinn Féin delegates were in prison. When Éamonn de Valera took over the position in April 1919, Brugha was appointed minister for defence as the war for Irish independence erupted. He opposed the

Anglo-Irish Treaty and joined the anti-Treaty forces as Civil War broke out. In July 1922, Brugha and a number of anti-Treaty forces were surrounded by members of the new Free State army in Hammon's Hotel on O'Connell Street, Dublin. On 3 July the commander of the Irish Free State forces in the area demanded the surrender of the hotel and its garrison. Brugha replied in Gaelic: 'Níl aon chuimhneamh agam ar a leithéid a dhéanamh' (I have no such intention). By 5 July the position had become untenable and as the building became engulfed in flames he ordered the remainder of his men to evacuate the hotel. With his pistol drawn, he calmly walked out the front door towards the waiting Free State soldiers. He was shot and seriously wounded, the bullet severing his femoral artery. Though he received immediate medical attention, he died from his wound two days later on 7 July in the Mater hospital, eleven days before his forty-eighth birthday. Controversy surrounds his death, as many believe his pistol was not loaded and he made no pretence of firing it. He is buried in Glasnevin cemetery. His death, like many others during the Civil War, left a void that would affect the political future of the country for decades to come.

Many of those who survived the 1916 Rising, the Irish War for Independence and the Civil War returned to a normal life despite having taken part in and witnessed the greatest of events – that of a country achieving its independence and taking its place amongst the other nations of the world.

Chapter 14

April 1916:
Military Success & Military Failure

> Apart from its general ultimate futility, the conduct
> of the insurrection showed great organisational ability
> and more military skill than had been attributed to
> the Volunteers.[68]

Urban warfare is a modern type of warfare conducted in
towns and cities. Before the twentieth century wars were
won or lost on open battlefields such as Waterloo and
Omdurman. Urban combat is very different from combat
in the open at operational and tactical levels.

The planning of the insurrection and the occupation of
the South Dublin Union is accredited to James Connolly
and Joseph Plunkett, but many questions have arisen in

relation to whether or not the plan was militarily sound. Why was the South Dublin Union chosen as a strong point and was it viable to occupy a complex of buildings that contained so many civilians?

From his positions within the Union and the outlying posts, Ceannt's task was to prevent troops from Richmond and Islandbridge barracks from entering the city. It is possible that Ceannt was also ordered to take and hold Kingsbridge Station. However, due to Eoin MacNeill's countermanding order, the 4th Battalion was seriously under strength and Ceannt could only deploy the men he had to the best of his ability. MacNeill's decision to countermand the order for a general mobilisation had a detrimental effect on the entire Rising, but especially on Ceannt's orders to hold the area in the vicinity of the Union. The area was vast and was impossible to hold with the small force that he had under his command, but he had the advantage of having a detailed knowledge of the grounds. In the weeks before the Rising the 4th Battalion had carried out manoeuvres that covered the exact positions occupied in the South Dublin Union.[69] Ceannt also reconnoitred the Union only days before his force occupied the position. He possessed drawings of the area and had pre-planned the defence.[70]

The South Dublin Union was a small city within a city and therefore provided a battleground that was favourable to the Irish Volunteers. Fighting in a built-up area such as the Union favoured the defenders who were the weaker force. Therefore, the complex was suitable for defence even though it covered over fifty acres. It was protected on two sides by part of the Grand Canal that has since been filled in and now carries part of Dublin's Luas or light rail network, and the complex was enclosed by a stone wall. It was well equipped with provisions and had its own bakery. The buildings offered cover and concealment to Ceannt's small force and, as a military commander, he knew his enemy must attack through the labyrinth of streets and alleyways that offered his men unlimited opportunities of killing grounds. His men occupied excellent vantage points throughout the battle, defending and attacking within their designated defensive zone. Ceannt and Brugha clearly defined areas of responsibility to their men on Easter Monday and these positions were mutually supporting to the their main headquarters at the Nurses' Home. Tunnelling through the buildings enabled a means of communication and escape to be established that resulted in a retreating force being able to regroup and fight again from a new strong-point. This form of action continued throughout the week.

Tactically, the siting of the defended Volunteer positions in relation to British barracks and points of advance was excellent.[71] The attacking force within this environment faced complications as they were entering a three-dimensional battle zone, where the buildings limited fields of view and fields of fire. Opportunities for concealment for the defending force were limitless even if they were inferior in number.[72] Ceannt's outposts were at Jameson's Distillery in Marrowbone Lane, Watkins' Brewery at Ardee Street and Roe's Distillery in Mount Brown.

Though the Volunteers were familiar with their area of operation, for a successful defence they would have needed a much larger force than was available on Monday 24 April, 1916. The military skill of the Irish Volunteers has often been overlooked in favour of their courage and sacrifice. Many Volunteers had been in training since the formation of the Irish Volunteers in 1913 and these dedicated young men and women were far superior soldiers to the raw recruits that arrived from England in the ranks of the 59th North Midland Division. The Volunteer officers, many of whom were ex-Fianna officers, were excellent marksmen, who had specialised training in the subject of street fighting in preparation for a rising in Dublin city. They were a dedicated force who believed in the cause of a republic. Volunteer Seamus Murphy recalls that in order to acquire rifles a scheme was introduced whereby each man contributed one shilling a week towards the purchase of a weapon. There was no difficulty in getting these subscriptions. The men gave up their little luxury of a pint or some other amenity in order to acquire arms.[73] The standard of leadership was high and this is reflected in the way the Volunteers fought with discipline, courage and determination. Excellent leadership greatly contributed to the morale of the Volunteers.

The ability of the Irish Volunteers to deceive the British into thinking that their force was numerous was perhaps the most important tactical plan contrived by Commandant Ceannt. Though the British had superior firepower, the Irish Volunteers utilised their limited resources to force the enemy to withdraw from battle on Monday and again on Thursday. The result of this tactic was that the South Dublin Union was not taken by force but was forced to surrender on orders from Patrick Pearse, the officer in command of the Irish Volunteers.

Controversy surrounds the order that was issued to retreat from the Nurses' Home, an order that left Brugha to defend the building on his own. Ceannt did not issue the order and though various people are named in witness statements, it still remains a mystery who ordered it.

Officers and men from both sides found the battle for the South Dublin Union a difficult experience:

I found a bullet in Dublin every bit as dangerous as a bullet in No-Man's Land. In some ways the fighting in Dublin was worse. In France you generally had a fair idea where the enemy was and where the bullets were going to come from. In Dublin you never knew when or from where you were going to be hit.[74]

Neither side knew exactly where the enemy was located and the battle lines were never fixed. Shots rang out in front, behind and on your flanks. British soldiers with battle experience found the network of narrow streets within the Union and the deadly guerrilla tactics of the Volunteers mentally exhausting.

Though the British military were taken by surprise by the insurrection, they reacted quickly and vigorously to the situation. The South Dublin Union garrison were one of the first Volunteer battalions to make contact with the enemy and there was no time to evacuate the staff and patients of the complex. However, provisions were made, such as moving them to safer quarters and identifying the buildings where they were quartered by draping Red Cross flags from the windows. This action by the staff of the Union, the Irish Volunteers and the British army greatly reduced the number of civilian casualties during the battle. Aware of the large number of civilians within the Union, Lowe did not deploy artillery there, instead concentrating his artillery forces nearer the centre of the city.

After their initial contact with the Irish Volunteers in the South Dublin Union on Monday 24 April, 1916, British crown forces attempted to storm the complex. Having gained entry to the Union at considerable loss, they failed to press home the attack, which resulted in the Volunteers regrouping and holding their positions. The decision to withdraw the Royal Irish Regiment at this early stage was to have a detrimental effect later in the week. Machine-gun and sniper fire from the Royal Hospital, Kilmainham, enabled the British to contain the Volunteer force within the Union. The method of utilising covering fire was textbook, as it provided cover for attacking infantry and kept down flanking fire. British tactics within the Union consisted of taking and occupying a block or building, clearing and securing it, and then moving onto the next one. This often involved fighting at close quarters, resulting in a heavy consumption of ammunition and also heavy casualties.[75]

When Brigadier General W.H.M. Lowe ascertained that the rebels had established themselves in various centres throughout the city, the first phase of operations he conducted was to attempt to isolate each group by forming a cordon of troops around their position. Having organised reinforcements from camps throughout Ireland, Brigadier General Lowe sent to England for the 59th North Midland Division. Lowe set a number of primary tasks that included the relief of Dublin Castle and the securing of the magazine fort and the vice-regal lodge, which ensured that the military contained and effectively bypassed the South Dublin Union. He concentrated his main force of action on taking the Volunteer headquarters at the General Post Office in Sackville Street, in order to destroy the control point of the Rising. To achieve this a line of posts was established from Kingsbridge Station (Heuston Station) along Thomas Street and Dame Street to Trinity College. The latter post was to become the main headquarters for the retaking of the city. Having secured this highway, British troops were able to enter the heart of the city and crown forces were in a strong position to launch their attack on the General Post Office.

Crushing the Rising in a built-up area within one week with new recruits and poorly trained soldiers was an impressive military achievement. Brigadier General Lowe's plans were successful and resulted in the unconditional surrender of the Irish Volunteers. However, while the general plan worked well, the British attack on the South Dublin Union on Thursday afternoon was a tactical error that had nothing to do with their overall strategy. Superior officers who failed to reconnoitre the area threw the inexperienced battalions of the Sherwood Forester Regiment into the fray. The use of fighting patrols and experienced officers and men from other regiments greatly reduced British casualties in this engagement, but there were alternative routes available which bypassed the Union and these should have been considered. The attack on the Union was a mistake that could have resulted in similar casualties as were suffered in the battle for Mount Street Bridge.

Some of the most bloody and decisive battles in recent times have been fought in towns and cities throughout the world. Today many military forces utilise the tactics and strategies that were deployed by both sides during the 1916 Rising. Many major battles were fought in the streets, houses and factories of Stalingrad in 1942, Warsaw in 1944 and Berlin in 1945. During the Korean War in 1950 there was severe fighting in Seoul. Between 1975 and 1982 Beirut became a battleground. In recent years as Yugoslavia descended into civil war, Sarajevo became a city of death as its streets came under fire from Serb forces. More recently, armies of occupation and civil power have been faced with the challenges of insurgency. This has been highlighted with the British and American involvement in Afghanistan and Iraq. Fighting in a built-up area is favoured by insurgent groups who can even the odds by drawing conventional infantry into a battlefield of high-rise buildings, sewers, houses and streets, thus reducing the disparity in combat power. The soldiers fighting in such an environment are under considerable stress and need special training for urban operations. The tactics of fighting and defence in a built-up area are still in their infancy, having only been developed in the early twentieth century. This form of warfare results in high civilian casualties and an increase in refugees. Fighting in a built-up area will continue to be a form of combat favoured by weaker forces.

EPILOGUE

All wars end; even this war will some day end, and the ruins will be rebuilt and the field full of death will grow food, and all this frontier of trouble will be forgotten. When the trenches are filled in, and the plough has gone over them, the ground will not long keep the look of war.[76]

Today, as the Luas light rail trundles through the grounds of the South Dublin Union, many passengers are unaware of the battles of 1916 that took place in this busy hospital complex. The memorial in the grounds of St James's Hospital to the Easter Rising is positioned in a prominent place close to the entrance, yet many people walk by unaware of the sacrifices that were made to ensure the freedom that we all enjoy today.

However, if one looks closely, there are many other memorials in the grounds in memory of these men. Many of the original buildings are hidden away amongst the urban development that accompanies any modern hospital, but they are still there, a testament to those who fought and died that Easter Week and also a testament to those who have preserved and conserved part of our historical heritage. In recent years, the development of Dublin city has threatened our connection to the past. High-rise structures dominate the city's skyline, casting a shadow across many historical buildings. The more famous of these buildings have been placed on the record of protected structures, brought about through a lengthy campaign by historians, conservationists and the public. Those involved should be commended for their actions, a struggle that almost mirrors our historic past.

On 14 December 1950, the Dáil debated the scheme for the rehabilitation and extension of St Kevin's Hospital. Dr C. Lehane asked for the removal of the unsightly walls surrounding the former South Dublin Union 'so that this anachronistic symbol of alien government may be abolished and the atmosphere which it creates dissipated'. Dr Noel Browne replied that a number of old stores and buildings had already been demolished and the demolition of the boundary walls was being considered. It was also suggested that the frontage of the hospital onto James's Street should be radically altered and a more attractive entrance constructed. New buildings for a new Ireland. In the years that followed, much of this work was carried out, but between the modern façades there remain to this day many links to our historical past. Conservation and preservation of these buildings is a fitting memorial to those on both sides who gave their lives in the battle for the South Dublin Union in 1916. The battle to protect and preserve the buildings within the Union still continues.

The names of those Irish Volunteers who were killed in action in the battle for the South Dublin Union are remembered in the street names of the nearby Corporation housing development that was constructed on McCaffrey's Estate, now known as Ceannt's Fort. This housing development was championed by W.T. Cosgrave in 1917 and is a fitting tribute to those who gave their lives in the cause for Irish independence.

The British soldiers who were killed in action are remembered in the Great War memorials that may be found hidden in churches and public buildings throughout Dublin city. Their names once forgotten, they are only now being recognised by a new generation as attitudes and opinions change and our involvement in the Great War is at last being acknowledged.

Those who survived the events of 1916, the Irish War of Independence and the tragedy of the Civil War, had an obligation to build again; not only to reconstruct a shattered country, but to build bridges amongst old adversaries, to teach others what they knew and to try, with what was left of their lives, to find and pass on to a new generation a goodness and meaning to this life. Today, we should try to continue this legacy.

Endnotes

1   Coakley, Professor D., *History of St James's Hospital* (www. stjames.ie/aboutthehospital/history)

2   Rees, R., *Ireland 1905-25: Vol. 1. Text & Historiography* (Colourprint Books, Newtownards, 1998)

3   MacNeill, E., *Dublin Sunday Independent* (23 April 1916)

4   Coughlan, J., Witness Statement W.S. 304 (Bureau of Military History 1913–1921, Dublin)

5   Cosgrave, W.T., Witness Statement File No. S.541, W.S 268 (Bureau of Military History 1913–1921, Dublin)

6   McCarthy, D., Witness Statement W.S. 1756 (Bureau of Military History 1913–1921, Dublin)

7   Doyle, P., *Reminiscences of Five Years Service of an Irish Volunteer* (Allen Library, Dublin)

8   Geoghegan, S., *The Campaigns & History of the Royal Irish Regiment, Vol. II* (William Blackwood & Sons, London, 1927)

9   Caulfield, M., *The Easter Rebellion* (Gill and Macmillan, Dublin, 1995)

10 Burke, J., Witness Statement W.S. 1758 (Bureau of Military History 1913–1921, Dublin)

11 Holland, R., Witness Statement, W.S. 280 (Bureau of Military History 1913–1921, Dublin)

12 Kenny J., Witness Statement W.S. 174 (Bureau of Military History 1913–1921, Dublin)

13 *Ibid.*

14 McCarthy, D., Witness Statement W.S. 1756 (Bureau of Military History 1913–1921, Dublin)

15 Volunteer, A, *The Capuchin Annual* (1966)

16 Joyce, J.V., *An t-Óglach, Conquering Blood* (12 June 1926)

17 *Ibid.*

18 Coughlan, J., Witness Statement W.S. 304 (Bureau of Military History 1913–1921 Dublin)

19 Murphy, W., Witness Statement W.S. 352 (Bureau of Military History 1913–1921, Dublin)

20 Caulfield, M., *The Easter Rebellion* (Gill & Macmillan, Dublin, 1995)

21 Geoghegan, S., *The Campaigns & History of the Royal Irish Regiment, Vol. II* (William Blackwood & Sons, London, 1927)

22 Bradbridge, E.U., *59th Division 1915–1918* (Wilfred Edmunds, Chesterfield, 1928)

23 Coughlan, J., Witness Statement W.S. 304 (Bureau of Military History 1913–1921, Dublin)

24 Cosgrave, W.T., Witness Statement File No. S.541, W.S. 268 (Bureau of Military History 1913–1921, Dublin)

25 Murphy, W., Witness Statement W.S. 352 (Bureau of

Military History 1913–1921, Dublin)

26 Mannion, A., Witness Statement W.S. 297 (Bureau of Military History 1913–1921, Dublin)

27 Geoghegan, S., *The Campaigns & History of the Royal Irish Regiment, Vol. II* (William Blackwood & Sons, London, 1927)

28 Ó Flaithbheartaigh, L., Witness Statement W.S. 248 (Bureau of Military History 1913-1921, Dublin)

29 Holland, R., Witness Statement W.S. 280 (Bureau of Military History 1913–1921, Dublin)

30 Oates, W.C., *The 2/8th Battalion,* The Sherwood Foresters in the Great War series (J&H Bell Ltd, Nottingham, 1921)

31 Vane, Sir F., *Agin the Government. Memories & Adventures of Sir Francis Fletcher Vane* (Br Sampson Low & Marston, London, 1929)

32 Oates, W.C., *The 2/8th Battalion,* The Sherwood Foresters in the Great War series (J&H Bell Ltd, Nottingham 1921)

33 Vane, Sir F., Letters to his Wife, April & May 1916. (Cumbria Record Office, The Castle, Carlisle)

34 Kenny J., Witness Statement W.S. 174 (Bureau of Military History 1913–1921, Dublin)

35 Coughlan, J., Witness Statement W.S. 304 (Bureau of Military History 1913–1921, Dublin)

36 Coakley, D., *Borderlands* (Elo Press Ltd, Dublin, 2002)

37 Joyce, J.V., *An t-Óglach, Conquering Blood* (12 June 1926)

38 Caulfield, M., *The Easter Rebellion* (Gill & Macmillan, Dublin, 1995)

39 Foran, J., Witness Statement W.S. 243 (Bureau of Military History 1913–1921, Dublin)

40 Oates, W.C., *The 2/8th Battalion*, The Sherwood Foresters in the Great War series (J&H Bell Ltd, Nottingham, 1921)

41 Gibbon, M., *Inglorious Soldier. An Autobiography*, (Hutchinson, London, 1968)

42 Smyth, P., Witness Statement W.S. 305 (Bureau of Military History 1913–1921, Dublin)

43 McCarthy, D., Witness Statement W.S. 1756 (Bureau of Military History 1913–1921, Dublin)

44 *Ibid.*

45 Holland, R., Witness Statement W.S. 280 (Bureau of Military History 1913–1921, Dublin)

46 Lowe, Brig. Gen. W.H.M., Reply to Pearse's letter of surrender (National Museum of Ireland, 1916)

47 Smyth, P., Witness Statement W.S. 305 (Bureau of Military History 1913–1921, Dublin)

48 Mac Lochlainn P.F., *Last Words* (Duchas, Dublin, 1990)

49 Burke, J., Witness Statement W.S. 1758 (Bureau of Military History 1913–1921, Dublin)

50 Vane, Sir F., Letters to his Wife April & May 1916. (Cumbria Record Office, The Castle, Carlisle)

51 PRO WO71/348

52 *Ibid.*

53 *Ibid.*

54 Mac Lochlainn P.F., *Last Words* (Duchas, Dublin, 1990)

55 *Ibid.*

56 Bradbridge, E.U., *59th Division 1915-1918* (Wilfred Edmunds, Chesterfield, 1928)

57 PRO WO71/348

58 PRO WO35/67/2

59 Maxwell, General Sir J.G., Memorandum, 11 May 1916, (Asquith Papers, MS43/26-33)

60 Kiberd, D., *1916 Rebellion Handbook* (The Mourne River Press, Dublin, 1998)

61 GDB/C004.03/0011 Guinness Archive, Diego Ireland

62 Kiberd, D., *1916 Rebellion Handbook* (The Mourne River Press, Dublin, 1998)

63 Tailyour H.W., *The Irish Times*, 16 June 1916

64 Maxwell, Sir J.G., Dispatch to War Office 21 July 1916

65 Maxwell, Sir J.G., General order issued to troops, 1 May 1916

66 Doyle, P., *Reminiscences of Five Years Service of an Irish Volunteer* (Allen Library, Dublin)

67 Vane, Sir F., *Agin the Government. Memories & Adventures of Sir Francis Fletcher Vane* (Br Sampson Low & Marston, London, 1929)

68 Nathan, Sir M., Royal Commission of Inquiry (London, 18 May)

69 Burke, J., Witness Statement W.S. 1758 (Bureau of Military History 1913–1921, Dublin)

70 Mannion, A., Witness Statement, W.S. 297 (Bureau of Military History 1913–1921, Dublin)

71 Hally, Col. P.J., 'The Easter 1916 Rising in Dublin: The Military Aspects', *The Irish Sword* (Dublin, 1966)

72   Holmes, R., *The Oxford Companion to Military History* (Oxford University press, Oxford, 2001)

73   Murphy, S., Witness Statement W.S. 1756 (Bureau of Military History 1913–1921, Dublin)

74   Martyn, Capt. M., Interview in M. Caulfield, *The Easter Rebellion* (Gill & Macmillan, Dublin, 1995)

75   Holmes, R., *The Oxford Companion to Military History*, (Oxford University Press, Oxford, 2001)

76   Masefield, J., *The Old Front Line* (Pen & Sword Books Ltd, Barnsley, 2003)

Index

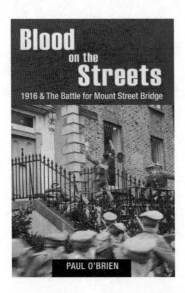

Blood on the Streets: 1916 & The Battle for Mount Street Bridge

Paul O'Brien

ISBN: 978 1 85635 576 6

Blood on the Streets explores what really happened during the battle for Mount Street Bridge. Based around the bridge over the canal at Mount Street, three well-positioned groups of Volunteers led by Lieutenant Michael Malone held out against a far greater number of British soldiers arriving from Dún Laoghaire. This book examines this battle and other events surrounding the Rising, and features the only written account by a British army officer of the executions at Kilmainham gaol in the aftermath of the Rising.

www.mercierpress.ie